FROM BROKEN TO BLESSED

How Simple Obedience to God Can Change Your Life

by DAVID G. PIPER

All Scripture references are from the New International Version of the Bible, copyright © 1973, 1978, 1984 by International Bible Society, Colorado Springs, Colorado, unless otherwise noted. References marked NKJV are from the New King James Version of the Bible, copyright © 1979, 1980, 1982 by Thomas Nelson, Inc., Nashville, Tennessee.

McDougal Publishing is a ministry of The McDougal Foundation, Inc., a Maryland nonprofit corporation dedicated to spreading the Gospel of the Lord Jesus Christ to as many people as possible in the shortest time possible.

Some of the names of people in this book have been changed for their protection or for their privacy.

Published by:

McDougal Publishing
P.O. Box 3595
Hagerstown, MD 21742-3595
www.mcdougalpublishing.com

ISBN 1-58158-056-8

Printed in the United States of America
For Worldwide Distribution

DEDICATION

I want to dedicate this book to the most important people in my life.

To my wife, Kecia, for being patient with me and at the same time loving me unconditionally as God continues to change me into the image of His Son.

To my two daughters, Megan and Savannah, because I am so proud of both of you, and I love you so much.

To Glen F. Piper, for being the best dad in the whole wide world.

To my grandparents, "Bigma" and "Pa" Piper and "Nanny" Snipes, for your continual prayers to Heaven which saved my life.

To my brother, Scott, because I love you more than words can say.

In memory of Ernestine Snipes Piper,
"Mama"
July 21, 1941—February 21, 1973

In memory of Elizabeth Nadine Piper,
"Bigma"
February 9, 1919—September 20, 2003

ACKNOWLEDGMENTS

Kecia, you are my wife, my best friend and my covenant partner in ministry and in life. I love you. You have sacrificed everything to help make our family, this ministry and me successful. You are a wonderful wife, a great mother and my number one intercessor.

Megan, thank you for your commitment to serve God with a pure heart. I love you and I am so very proud of the young lady you are growing up to be.

Savannah, thank you for being patient with me. It is my heart's desire to be a good father and a great friend to you.

Daddy, thanks for everything you are and everything you continue to do for me. I love you so very much.

Pastor Benny and Suzanne Hinn, thank you for paying the price to take God's healing and saving power to the world. Because of your obedience to Him, I am now walking out God's destiny for my life totally free from the bondage of Satan.

A special thanks to Paul and Linda McGrath for standing by my side from the time we met at O.C.C. in Orlando until now.

Thank you to David and Ginny Alsobrook for being real, true friends and for all of your encouraging words.

Thank you to my pastor, Mike Hobbs, for being both pastor and friend to me.

Thank you to my father-in-law, Pastor Elmer Golden, for believing in the call of God on my life when very few others did.

Thanks, Pastor Stan, for "Thirsty Thursdays."

Thanks to Lashea for being my mighty prayer warrior during the tough times and for being the greatest sister-in-law in the world.

Thank you, Keith Griffis, for everything you have done for me and my family and ministry.

A special thanks to Pastor Larry Mauriello for standing up for me as well as being there for me at all times.

Thank you, Pastors William and Lisa Hancock and all the family at House of Praise, for all that you continue to do for this ministry.

Thank you, Uncle Harold and Aunt Frances, for loving me unconditionally. I love both of you more than you will ever know.

Thank you, Norma Jean. You will always hold a special place in my heart. I love you.

Thank you, Ralph Hocutt, for meeting me at the tree in your backyard in 1988. That was the beginning of what I am today.

Thank you, Jeanette Biesecker, for helping to make this book a reality. You are truly an anointed vessel of God.

Thanks to everyone else, pastors, ministry partners and prayer warriors, whom God has placed in my life. Your prayers and support sustain us. You know who you are, and more importantly, He knows who you are. Without you, this book would not be touching the world for Jesus Christ.

CONTENTS

FOREWORD

In this exciting book you will see that David Piper was no saint but rather an average guy who failed repeatedly. David could not break the cycle of drug addiction through twelve-step programs and psychological treatments, but God, who is rich in mercy, set him free and established his feet on the path of righteousness by teaching him the basic principles of obedience.

Today, David Piper lives a consistent Christian life because of the power of God in his life. Perhaps it is because the reality of God's grace and delivering power is so real in his own life that David is able to believe God for the many he lays hands on today. Miracles happen in his meetings. David sincerely gives God the glory for everything that happens in them, and the unusual and extraordinary often does happen.

The first time I saw David Piper, the Lord spoke to me that he was called to do the works of God in the nations of the world. Since then I have had the privilege of attending his services and receiving his prayers. My sense of hearing had diminished somewhat, but after David prayed for me I could hear much better. More importantly, my wife was healed of neck and back pain that had bothered her day and night. God uses this young man and has given him an unusual boldness to do the works of God.

Reading his book is exciting and God glorifying. David doesn't whitewash his past, but lets it all out so that readers can find help through the same grace Jesus offers all. Your faith will be built up reading his story. It is with great joy that I recommend this book and this man's ministry to everyone everywhere in Jesus' name!

David Alsobrook
Nashville, Tennessee

Introduction

But seek first his kingdom and his righteousness, and all these things will be given to you as well.

Matthew 6:33

My flight landed in Jacksonville, Florida, on a Thursday evening. My associate, Jimmy, and I had just returned from an exciting ministry trip to Nigeria. We couldn't wait to tell our wives all of the marvelous, miraculous things God had done on this trip. That night at home, I told Kecia, my wife, about all of the amazing things God had done on this trip. There were so many miracles that I didn't know where to begin telling her about them. God had given us many words and instructions. Because of our love for Him and our hunger to be used by Him, we did everything God told us to do, and the results were many miracles of healing, deliverance, provision and much more. The trip had been as extraordinary as my life had become over the past few years.

The next day, Kecia and I drove to Atlanta. We needed some quality time alone and had decided to stay at one of our favorite hotels there. When we got to the hotel, the clerk at the front desk told us she was going to upgrade our $69.00 a night room to the largest suite they had. I hesitated, thinking it was going to cost me a whole lot more money. But the clerk assured me that there was no extra cost to us. I was dumbfounded. I didn't say anything else except, "Thank You, Lord."

When we got to the tenth floor of this five-star hotel, we walked into a room that was close to one thousand square feet and had two bathrooms with marble floors, huge closets, a kitchen, a couch, an oak bed with a canopy, and windows that went all the way around the room. God said, "Welcome to the place of obedience."

Wow! Here was the Father showering unexpected blessing on me, an ex-drug addict Georgia country boy, showing me the results of simple obedience. I was now living an extraordinary life, one far more fulfilling and exciting than I had ever dreamed possible, and I was now receiving the benefits that come with that life. It had taken me many years to come to this "place of obedience" in my life, and the road to getting there had been very rocky.

God had shown me His desire for my life at a young age, but I had grown rebellious as a youth and walked away from it. In the years that followed, I learned the results of disobedience the hard way. I wanted to do what I wanted to do and didn't care what anyone else thought. That attitude had cost me nearly everything I had. But God didn't let me get away from Him so easily. He crushed me like a bug, put a U-turn in my life, and set me back on the path of obedience.

Now here I was in an upscale Atlanta hotel suite, receiving an outpouring of God's blessings. I had learned the importance of an obedient life, and I had finally learned how to be so hungry for Him that I was willing to abide in total submission to Him.

God's blessings aren't just for me; they're for all of His children. God loves His children. He wants to give us all an extraordinary Christian life. The key to receiving that is learning to obey both God's Word and the leading of the Holy Spirit.

There's really no secret to getting to a place in your life where God continually blesses you, but the journey to get there is required of everyone who calls God "Father." It's my desire to help others learn how to walk the path of obedience so that they too can experience God's showers of blessings.

CHAPTER ONE

THE CALL TO OBEDIENCE

"Before I formed you in the womb I knew you, before you were born I set you apart; I appointed you as a prophet to the nations."
"Ah, Sovereign LORD," I said, "I do not know how to speak; I am only a child."
But the LORD said to me, "Do not say, 'I am only a child.' You must go to everyone I send you to and say whatever I command you. Do not be afraid of them, for I am with you and will rescue you," declares the LORD.   Jeremiah 1:5-8

The prophet Jeremiah was just a youth when God called him to begin serving as a prophet of God, but even before he was born, God had already planned out the purpose for Jeremiah's life. God's Word tells us it was the same in the life of Moses, the life of David, the life of John the Baptist and even the life of Jesus Himself. But this scripture tells us that Jeremiah wasn't ever going to experience the fulfillment of that plan unless he learned one simple thing—obedience. God promised He would be with Jeremiah and would rescue him *only if* he would obey those things God told him to do.

Many Christians don't understand that "only if" is part of the contract God makes with His people. Even before we're fully formed in our mothers' wombs, God has made a plan for us and has decided on a purpose for our lives. At some point in our lives, we choose either God's plan or our own plan. If we choose God's plan, we begin down the path of obedience by repenting of our sins and accepting God's gift of Jesus Christ to save us.

When we become the children of God through salvation in Christ, that involves surrendering our wills over to Him. We consciously make a choice to live our lives obedient to His will rather than our own. This qualifies us to receive His blessings and protection, but that's "only if" we're obedient to Him. Not one of us will experience the fulfillment of the plan for our lives unless we learn that one simple thing—obedience to those things God has called us to do.

One reason this is important is because our obedience is the evidence of our love for Him. Now, this statement is not my measuring stick; it's *God's* measuring stick. Jesus says in John 14:15, *"If you love me, you will obey what I command."* Jesus uses our obedience as proof of our love for Him. When we walk in disobedience, we show disrespect for His authority over us.

This is true in all parent/child relationships. I have two beautiful daughters, Megan and Savannah. If I give one of my girls instructions to do something and that child stands up to me and tells me "no," or she deliberately does something other than what she was told, she is showing me disrespect. When my daughters tell me they love me and then disobey me or ignore my instructions, their behavior does not back up their words. The words and the actions are in conflict, and the actions don't show me love. Disrespect doesn't represent love. Love is represented in our actions. And so, our disobedience to God is also disrespect and doesn't represent love.

In God's eyes, our obedience is also evidence that we love our brothers and sisters in Christ.

> *This is how we know that we love the children of God:*
> *by loving God and carrying out his commands.*
>   1 *John 5:2*

We find an example of this truth in Jesus' encounter with the rich man in the Gospel of Matthew, chapter 19. This might be a new take on this scripture for you, but just bear with me.

In this scripture, a rich young man comes to Jesus and asks Him how he can have eternal life. Jesus tells him to obey the commandments. The young man asks Jesus which ones. From his question, we can see already that the young man is starting to hold back. Jesus names off some of the ten commandments along with His own commandment of *love your neighbor as yourself.* Take special note as to which commandments Jesus lists. He names only those commandments that pertain to how we should treat other people. It's not accidental here that the Lord doesn't name all ten of the commandments given to Moses. He's specifically targeting this young man's relations with others.

The young fellow tells the Lord that he's already obeying these commandments. He then goes another step to ask what else he needs to do. This is where his real test comes. Jesus instructs him to sell all of his possessions and give to the poor. Now keep in mind that this is the Lord Jesus Christ giving the young man this instruction, so this is not optional. Obedience is required.

Jesus was testing the truth of the young man's assertion that he was already obeying all those commandments on how to treat others. Jesus was expecting this young man to show his love for others through the action of giving over his wealth to those who were in need. The result is that the guy just can't part with his wealth. He turns and goes away sad.

Rather than give what he has to the poor, rather than obey the command of Christ, the young man walks away. His inability to part with his wealth and give to the poor is evidence that he lacks love for others. And his inability to obey Jesus is evidence that he lacks love for God.

At this point, you might be thinking, *Doesn't God love us no matter what?* The answer is definitely "yes"! God will always love us, in both obedience and disobedience. His love is unconditional. But His blessings are not, and that's a third reason why it's important to obey God. Our obedience is connected to our receiving the blessings of God promised in His Word to His children.

If we're not obedient, we don't get God's blessings. Our obedience is connected to our being blessed. God did not make us to be like robots. He's not going to force us to do anything, but He gives everyone a free will and a choice. We all have the opportunity to say "yes" to God, or we can say "no." But the answer we give Him determines whether or not we experience all of God's fullness and whether or not we receive the immeasurable blessings of Heaven.

On the other end, our disobedience is connected

with our being disciplined and corrected by God. When we walk in our own wills and ways, the Lord will let us suffer the consequences of our choices. He won't rescue us from the results of what we've sown.

One last reason for being obedient to God is simply because of who He is. He's the One with power over life and death, Heaven and Hell. God is our Creator, and it is pure foolishness for the creation to buck against the Creator when that Creator has the power to make you or break you, to take you to Heaven or cast you into Hell. "The fear of the Lord" may sound like an old-fashioned Pentecostal term to some believers, but in these last days the meaning of that term is going to become clearer to us as He reveals more and more of Himself to the world.

So adding it all up, obedience to God is evidence that we love Him, evidence that we love others, necessary to receive all of the blessings promised in God's Word, and required because of who God is.

Given all of these reasons for obedience to God, why is it that so many of us still choose the path of disobedience?

Chapter Two

The Path of Disobedience

There is a way that seems right to a man, but in the end it leads to death. Proverbs 14:12

Disobedience to God is an old, old story. It goes right back to the very beginning in the Garden of Eden when Adam and Eve disobeyed a direct command: "Do not eat the fruit of THAT tree or you will die." God had made the consequences very clear. The first two people ever created had had everything going for them, so why risk all the benefits of obedience in order to exercise a little self-will?

Following that first act of disobedience, things didn't change much down through the ages after that. There are plenty of examples of disobedience to God in the Old Testament: Lot's wife's looking back at Sodom and Gomorrah, Aaron's building of the golden calf, Korah's rebelling against the leadership of Moses, Achan's stealing booty from the victory at Jericho, Jonah's refusing to prophesy to Nineveh, and lots of others.

The prime example of what happens when we disobey God is found in the history of the nation of Israel itself. From the time that God took Israel as His chosen people, He made it clear to them what He expected of them. He told them exactly what the benefits of obeying Him were and also what the results of disobeying Him were. (See Leviticus 26.) But consistently throughout her history, Israel failed to remain obedient to the Lord. God finally scattered the people of Israel among their enemies. Israel had chosen to go down the path of disobedience and reaped the consequences.

Now, God didn't leave Israel without hope. He left an open door for them by promising that He would restore them if they would repent and begin to walk in obedience again. And there were times in Israel's history when the children of Israel did turn things around. Even after they had been scattered abroad, when they began to repent, God honored His promise by bringing them back to the Promised Land. In the times when they repented and started walking in obedience, they began to experience God's blessings again.

The principles of obeying and disobeying are still the same today: Obey God, get blessed; disobey God, get consequences.

My own life is a classic example of the consequences of disobedience. Before I took that first step of obedience to God, which is repentance, my life was an extreme example of what happens when you start down the path of disobedience.

I had actually started out life very much like the prophet Jeremiah had. God had shown me the calling on my life at a very young age. I grew up in a church-going family in the state of Georgia. My mother had died when I was only nine, so I lived with my grandparents for a few years.

One day when I was twelve, my grandmother took me to a little country church where I received a prophetic word from a visiting evangelist. A married couple, Jack and Mary Wells, were holding evangelistic services there, and Mary Wells prophesied over me that I would one day preach the Gospel and have a world-wide ministry with signs, wonders and miracles following. She told me I would one day be just like the apostle Paul. And I was only twelve when she gave me this word! But at the time I didn't know about the "only if" clause that went with that promise of God, and the enemy knew the call and the anointing that was on my life.

Some of us walk around believing that God is obligated to fulfill every prophetic promise given to us regardless of our actions, but that couldn't be further from the truth. God's prophetic word to each of us is a promise of what *can be* if you and I walk in obedience. God isn't going to make a preacher out of a crack-smoking, cocaine snorting misfit *unless* that misfit takes that first step of obedience. That step is *repentance*.

I wasn't willing to take that first step of obedience until I was thirty-four. The years between twelve and thirty-four are not ones I would wish to live over again. Another, stronger word for disobedience is *rebellion*, and that's where I was during those twenty-two years of my life—in rebellion.

In the time following that prophetic word, some profound changes took place in my life. My father had re-married a Christian lady who lived on a farm. I went to live with them. My uncle and aunt, Harold and Frances Sikes, began to help raise me along with my dad and stepmother. In these years, I became a rebellious kid with no friends. Other kids would pick on me all the time. Even after school I remember going home all by myself, being lonely and having nothing. I spent the afternoons when I wasn't working on the farm with

Uncle Harold alone in the woods with my rifle. At fourteen I fell into using marijuana, drugs and alcohol.

My family tried hard to raise me in a right relationship with the Lord. Every time the church door was open we were there, but I refused to obey. I was given the choice to either get my act together or leave. I paid no attention to their ultimatum. Then the day came when my parents couldn't handle me any longer and sent me back to live with my grandparents again.

My grandparents lived in a town named Poulan, near Sylvester. Poulan was a small town where everybody knew everybody else.

At the high school there I didn't hang around the football players, cheerleaders or preppies. I'd hang around the kids who would pay attention to me—the smokers and the druggies. These were the kids that people considered to be "trash." But those were the kids who accepted me, and I ended up with the same addictions they had.

Over the next seventeen and a half years I tried nearly every illegal drug out there, and I became addicted to crack cocaine, alcohol and tobacco. Crack is just about the worst drug that you can get addicted to. I stole money from others to pay for my habit. I forged checks. I sold drugs to other junkies. Everyone in the Poulan/Sylvester area knew I was trouble.

By the time all was said and done, I had lost everything. I had lost my wife, my kid, my home, my reputation in the community, and my rights from the government. I couldn't even vote. I even spent time in jail and time in mental institutions. I had received thirty-eight years of probation from the state of Georgia. I wasn't allowed to leave the state without permission.

In the Psalms, King David called the dark part of his

life "miry clay." My life was about as "miry" as it could get. I knew right from wrong. I knew God's Word and was fully aware of what I should have been doing. But every time the Holy Spirit would come to me to try to draw me to Him, I would turn a deaf ear. I walked the path of disobedience right down to the place of brokenness. Some people call the experience of that place "hitting bottom."

For some of us, "hitting bottom" is the only cure for disobedience. There are two kinds of people at "the bottom": the people God is making and the people God is breaking. You see, God will break you before He can make you.

Did you ever play with Play-Doh when you were a kid? If you did, you know that you get a small, colorful lump of soft Play-Doh inside a cylinder-shaped container. While the Play-Doh is protected inside the container, it stays soft. That's how we are when we're willing to submit to God's rulership—soft and ready for Him to shape us into the image of Jesus. If you leave that lump of Play-Doh sit outside of the container too long, it begins to get hard—too hard to shape it into anything. This is what happens to us when we remain outside of God's protective covering. When we live in disobedience, we become like that lump of hardened Play-Doh.

So what happens when you take that hardened lump of Play-Doh and smash it against a rock? It will break up into pieces. When you break it down into smaller pieces, you can start adding water to them and slowly start working the Play-Doh around in your hands again. The Play-Doh gradually begins to soften up until you're able to shape and mold it again.

You could try to soften that lump of Play-Doh while it's all in one piece, but it takes a lot longer and the Play-

Doh is much harder to work. If you break it up into smaller pieces, the process of softening it becomes much easier and quicker.

God lets disobedient people get broken at the bottom so He can start adding living water to the smaller pieces. Then He begins shaping them into something good, something He can use.

If you're not willing to be made into something new, you're likely to be stuck at "the bottom" forever or until it "leads to death."

About three years ago, a friend called me and said, "David, my brother Joey (not his real name) took an overdose. Would you come pray for him? We're believing that God will do for him what He did for you."

It wasn't Joey's first overdose. He'd OD'd so often before that he had learned exactly how many pills he could take to get to the point of death without actually dying. The ambulance would always come get him. Sometimes they would have to pump his stomach, and sometimes he'd end up in rehab. He was living in a vicious circle of hitting bottom over and again.

I went with his sister over to Joey's house. The place was dark and smoky—exactly what you'd find in a drug-infested atmosphere. Joey was lying in bed with the covers pulled up to his neck. Beside the bed were the empty pill bottles and liquor bottles. We opened up the windows and doors and started praying over him, and I mean praying hard.

Joey came around and sobered up right before our eyes. This time he realized he'd come just a hair too close to the edge of death. He made a commitment right then to turn his life around, and he asked Jesus to save him. He quit doing drugs and starting living right again.

After some time he didn't look like the same person.

He'd changed. Even his house didn't look the same any more. I thought he'd finally gotten his life right.

Unfortunately, it didn't last. I recently got an e-mail from his sister. I opened it up and saw Joey's obituary. Shocked, I called his sister and asked her what had happened. She told me, "David, he was in a drug dealer's house. The drug dealer had to call the ambulance to come and get him."

Joey had made a conscious choice to go back into his old habits and lifestyle. When God brings you out of the place of brokenness and gives you a new life, don't go back to your old ways, "for in the end it leads to death."

The place of brokenness was never intended to be a deadend, nor was it meant for repeated visits; it was meant to be a U-turn. And the only way to begin to make a U-turn into a right life with God is to take that first step of obedience—repentance.

CHAPTER THREE

TAKING THE FIRST STEP

Hear my prayer, O LORD; let my cry for help come to you. Do not hide your face from me when I am in distress. Turn your ear to me; when I call, answer me quickly.   Psalm 102:1-2

That slide to the bottom can be short and fast or long and slow, so making the U-turn can be either a quick experience or a long, drawn-out process. In either case, it is a battle that is fiercely fought. My friend's brother Joey was never able to completely get around that bend, and he lost his battle.

The Christian life is more than a one-step-to-victory deal. Finding salvation is wonderful, but it's just the beginning to obtaining an extraordinary life. It's learning to hear God and obey His Word and His voice day by day, hour by hour, minute by minute. You don't work to get salvation—that's free through the shed blood of Jesus—but you do work after salvation. The Word of God says:

Do your best to present yourself to God as one approved, a workman who does not need to be ashamed

> *and who correctly handles the word of truth.*
> 2 Timothy 2:15

It takes training to walk the path of obedience, just as a marathon runner needs daily training to run a race. We need to learn the Word, we need to spend time in prayer, and we also need one other key ingredient that has often been missing in the Body of Christ in the past: discipleship.

Without other, more mature believers to mentor us and to walk alongside us, the dangers of failing are great. I suspect a lack of discipleship had a lot to do with Joey's fall and eventual death. I was very familiar with the struggle Joey had faced. I had lived it myself.

In my own life, it took about two years to get right and stay right with God. By 1996, my life was such a mess that my druggie friends didn't even want to hang around me. You know you're in serious trouble when you have a pocket full of drugs that you're willing to share but your druggie friends don't want to be near you.

Besides the addictions, my lifestyle up to this point included near-death experiences, periodic jail time, one job after another and satanic worship. But just to show you how God will work when your time at the bottom is over, I'll tell you the amazing things the Lord did to finally bring me to that first step of obedience—repentance.

I found work as a waiter at that time in the only restaurant left in town that would hire me—a restaurant where the Christians in town frequently ate. As I was on my way to work one morning, something happened. Even though I wasn't saved at the time, the Holy Spirit came to me and reminded me of those words prophesied to me when I was twelve. After that I wasn't able to get that prophecy out of my mind.

Mary Wells, the evangelist who'd given me that word, had expressly said that it would be twenty-two years before God fulfilled that prophecy, and I was now nearing the end of that twenty-two year wait.

In July of that year, my grandmother invited me to go to church with her. My grandmother was a fierce prayer warrior for all of her grandchildren. My grandmother was also very smart. She knew I would never agree to go if she asked me herself. Instead, she sent my cousin Vanessa to ask me. She knew I would listen to Vanessa. When my cousin told me that Jack and Mary Wells would be preaching that night, I agreed to go to church.

I remember that night so clearly. I sat in the back on the right side of the church and wiped the tears from my eyes as my cousin sang "His Eye Is on the Sparrow" during the worship.

The Holy Spirit had begun to break apart some of the hardness of my heart. I didn't accept Jesus that night, but lots of water was poured on that dormant seed inside of me, and that seed was now beginning to germinate.

Jack Wells came to me privately in the back of the church and invited me to another one of his services in Lenox, a nearby town, on Sunday. He then prayed over me that the desire to do drugs would leave me. Something happened in me right then, because when I left there that night, I had no cravings for crack or any other drug, at least for that night.

I began to think about how I could get off work on Sunday to go to the service where Jack and Mary would be ministering. Sunday was the busiest day of the week in the restaurant where I worked because all of the Christians in town came there for Sunday dinner and we would be very busy all day. It would be nearly impossible for me to get off to go to church. Everyone on staff wanted Sunday off, and I was low man on the totem pole there. I had never had a Sunday off before. I also didn't have any money to pay for the gas to get to Lenox.

I prayed sincerely for the first time in years. I prayed, "God, if You are listening to me and You really want me in that service on Sunday, then arrange it so I will be able to leave work in time to get there, and give me enough money for the trip."

When I went into work on Sunday morning, my head waitress told me the bosses had decided to let me off work early if I would work the smoking section of the restaurant. One part of my prayer seemed to be answered, but working the smoking section would make the other part more difficult.

The smoking section was the worst section for making money. Because our customers were nearly all Christians, they didn't smoke or wouldn't smoke in front of other Christians. It would be difficult to make enough tips to have the money to go to the service in Lenox.

To the amazement of all the waitresses and myself, my section remained packed with customers all day. One waitress even accused me of making customers sit in the smoking section, but I had no hand in it. I knew it was God telling me He wanted me in that service. I made more money on that lunch shift than I had ever made on any other Sunday lunch shift. I was off work early that day and in my car headed for Lenox by four o'clock. The Lord had cleared the way for me to follow the call I was sensing.

I stopped on the way to church to buy a case of beer. Even though beer sales were illegal on Sunday, I could always find a way to get it if I wanted it. As I drove, I opened up a can, took a few swallows and threw it out the window. It was the worst tasting beer I'd ever had. I tried several more cans, with the same result. I wasn't able to take pleasure in my vice. God was still working.

That night in the Lenox service, I sat in the center of the church, smelling like a brewery. But no one commented on it or told me to leave. They loved me anyway.

The evangelist was moving and operating in God's power. He was stirring the church, and he stirred me. I was broken and tired of the life I was leading. I ran to the altar during the altar call that evening and gave my life over to Jesus.

When I left the church that night, I remember the whole world seemed different somehow. Colors were brighter. Sounds were clearer. Everything seemed new to me. It was unlike any high I had ever experienced. It was a clean feeling, like a cool breeze flowing through and over my body. I drove home that evening watching the July summer sun set on the horizon, noticing the beauty of it for the first time in many years. It was July 17, 1996, and I had been born again.

At the restaurant the next day, God used me to heal a little boy. This was the first miracle of many healing miracles to come. A mother and a grandmother had come in for lunch with a little boy around four or five years old. I heard the Holy Spirit tell me that the little boy was sick and that I was to pray for him.

The three of them were all dressed up. When I asked why, they told me they were going to the doctor to get a foot brace for the boy. The child had a crooked foot that had been deformed since birth. I asked them if they believed God could heal the boy's foot.

The mother wasn't sure, but the grandmother, said, "I believe He can." I asked for permission to pray for the little boy's foot. They were amazed that their waiter was even having this conversation with them, but they agreed.

I bent down, took the boy's crooked foot in my hands, and prayed very simply, "Father, You told me to pray for this boy's foot, so please heal this little boy. Amen." I told them that when they got to the doctor, he would tell them the boy was healed, and then I went back to waiting tables.

About a month later, the ladies and the child came back to the restaurant. "Guess what?" they said. "When we got to the doctor, the nurse removed his shoe and his foot was perfect!" I then looked at the mother and told her that Jesus wanted her heart. With tears in her eyes, she let me lead her to Jesus in prayer.

That was only the beginning of what God would work through me, but the enemy was still working too. It was his plan to derail me before I could make the U-turn in my life onto that path of obedience.

On the night I had given my life to Jesus, I had taken my first step of obedience and had begun my rise from the bottom of my life, but it wasn't my departure from the place of brokenness yet.

In spite of my conversion and the miracle healing of the little boy, the enemy was still lying in wait for me. The same old desires were still there along with the same old friends (and even some new ones) to encourage me to give in to those desires. I had no discipling elsewhere in my life to help me fend off my "old man."

I knew I was struggling and failing, so I tried some of

the twelve-step programs that were available to me. I got a sponsor, and these programs became my whole life. But the programs weren't a cure for our addictions. In fact, the programs taught that there was no cure for addictions. We would sit in our meetings, talk about the "higher power" and confess with our mouths that we would never be cured. The programs can keep you away from alcohol and drugs for a time, but they've never set anyone free.

The next two years of my life were a yo-yo type of existence. The twelve-step programs convinced me that I would always be an addict. And I had no one from the church to teach me the ways of God or hold me accountable. Given those things, it should have been no big surprise when I began messing my life up again. It was Satan's plan to derail me before I could make the U-turn in my life onto that path of obedience.

Satan's traps aren't especially designed for me alone. It's his plan to derail all those who accept Jesus. Oftentimes new believers will almost immediately experience an attack of Satan in an attempt to steal their newly found faith. Jesus said in His own words:

> *"Some people are like seed along the path, where the word is sown. As soon as they hear it, Satan comes and takes away the word that was sown in them."*
>
> Mark 4:15

But once a man or woman accepts Jesus as Savior and becomes a child of God, the Lord doesn't leave that person alone or helpless to face temptations and trials.

> *No temptation has seized you except what is common to man. And God is faithful; he will not let you be*

> *tempted beyond what you can bear. But when you are*
> *tempted, he will also provide a way out so that you*
> *can stand up under it.* 1 Corinthians 10:13

God always makes a way for us to overcome temptations and to stand up under trials. Satan's attacks on us become restrained by God so that the troubles we go through become part of the refining process God begins in our lives rather than being the end of us.

God begins transforming us into a whole new person. We're placed in circumstances that try us and stretch us so that God can teach us how to begin making the right choices.

It's in learning to make those right choices—learning to obey God—that we are able to make the U-turn in the road and start on the path of obedience.

Chapter Four

Making the U-turn

My son, do not despise the LORD's discipline and do not resent his rebuke, because the LORD disciplines those he loves, as a father the son he delights in.

Proverbs 3:11, 12

When God begins that training process in us to teach us obedience, some of us catch on early in the process, but some of us don't and then that refining process often involves discipline in order to direct us back to the right choices.

God will not play games with you once you've turned your life over to Him. If you start treating your life like it's your own again, He *will* discipline you. You can sin successfully when you're not saved, but once you accept Jesus into your heart, you can never sin successfully. God will hold you accountable. There's a responsibility that comes with giving your life to Jesus. You are now bearing His name and carrying His Spirit, and the Lord will hold you accountable for treating His name and housing His Spirit in a manner that's worthy of Him.

Just as a horse trainer uses a bit that applies pressure in the mouth of the horse in order to guide the animal, God uses discipline that applies pressure in our lives to guide us in the direction He wants us to go. Horses gradually learn to obey directional commands with less and less pressure, and so do we. Without that "bit in the mouth" (God's discipline) to train us, we end up being chased through life instead of being led.

When you surrender to God and begin to walk in obedience, you're being led by Him. But when you take your eyes off Him and let your circumstances in the natural rule over you, you're being chased—chased by the world, chased by the devil, chased by your addictions, chased by your weaknesses. Something other than God has control over your life.

One thing we need to understand in order to grasp this is that we, as humans, at no point have control over anything. We never did and we never will. Those who believe they do are deceived.

Our lives are either controlled by God, or controlled by other things such as money, fame, a desire for power, or whatever we have made to be our god in the place of God. So if you are not led by God, you are being chased by your particular circumstances.

When the prophet Elijah was facing off in his showdown with the prophets of Baal, he was being led by God. When he was running for his life in fear of Jezebel, he was being chased by his circumstances. He had taken his eyes off God long enough to shake his faith. God wasn't the one who told Elijah to go hide in the cave.

To be led by God requires giving Him complete control, and giving Him complete control requires obedience to the commands in His Word and to the leading of His Spirit.

I had given my life to Jesus in that evangelistic service. I had accepted Him as my Savior. And God used me in a moment of obedience, such as when the little boy's foot was healed, but I was still being chased by my circumstances. Consequently, God began to apply discipline to my life.

It took me a long time to get my life right even after I accepted Jesus. I fell into the vicious circle of using drugs again. My rational thinking became messed up and I began to feel a sense of desperation. I knew I had broken my probation and that it would only be a matter of time before I was caught. Because I didn't want to go back to jail, I thought I could avoid that by committing myself to a mental hospital.

I had been in the mental hospital before, but this time it was different. They didn't put me in the thirty-day program I'd been in before—this time they put me in lockdown. This was the area where they kept people who were violent and were dangerous to themselves and others. Some of them had even committed murder or other violent crimes.

There was nothing to do in lockdown but walk around in circles. I remained in lockdown twenty-four hours a day, but in spite of having sought refuge in the hospital, the law caught up with me anyway. My probation officer, Guerry Phillips, had put out a warrant for my arrest due to the probation violation. The sheriff's office came for me at the hospital and took me right out of lockdown there straight to lockdown in the county jail. A hearing was soon scheduled for me to go before the superior court judge.

Because I thought the hearing would go better for me if it looked like I was mentally unstable, I decided to lie to the doctors, who were still treating me. I thought I could plead insanity, so I told them I was hearing voices.

The doctors started treating me with so much medication that I really did start hearing voices. They weren't sure what dosages to give me. It was all I could manage just to walk around. I couldn't function mentally or make logical decisions. The medicines so intoxicated my body that my mind wasn't entirely there. I was like a zombie.

During the time I spent in jail, I think I saw daylight maybe two times. There was a little window in my room, but it wasn't really big enough to see anything through it.

Life was so bad in the jail that I threatened to kill myself, hoping they would send me back to the mental hospital. Instead they placed me in isolation, where I was stripped naked and had to eat without utensils. This was so I could not harm myself with them.

To get out of isolation, I spent twelve hours confessing that I didn't want to kill myself, that I had only said that so they would send me back to the hospital. They finally believed me and moved me back to the regular cell. The whole time all of this was going on, I was still on the medications being administered by the doctors from the hospital.

I had reached a place where I didn't think God could help me. I'd been told that I would be in jail until my court hearing, which would be somewhere around ninety to one hundred days from my incarceration, and that hard time in prison would be the likely result of that hearing. By violating my probation, I was facing the possibility of thirty years in a state penitentiary.

Then one day something happened. I heard the words of "Amazing Grace" being sung in another room. *Amazing grace—how sweet the sound—that saved a wretch like me*! I began to feel God in the place.

Some of the other inmates were attending a once-a-week church service held in the jail and had suggested from time to time that I come to it. But I had told them that I didn't believe it could help me because I'd made so many mistakes. I was wallowing in so much self-pity and guilt that I didn't believe God cared enough about me to help me.

However, on the day that I heard "Amazing Grace" I changed my mind about going to the service. I slipped into the room and sat on the floor.

All I remember about the service that night was that the preacher had us stand up and stick our arms straight out. He slapped each one of us on the wrist, commanding in the name of Jesus that all our bonds be loosed and broken.

The preacher told us that God was going to begin working miracles in our lives that very night. Some of us would be granted an early release as well as favor with the courts.

This service was the beginning point of my climb up from the bottom of my life. God then began to do a series of miracles to get me out of trouble.

The next day I began to talk to God again. With my hands raised toward Heaven, I sought His forgiveness for my disobedience and asked Him to help me out of the circumstances I was trapped in. I felt a blanket of warmth wrap around me as confirmation of His love and reassurance.

Now that I was right with God again, I wanted a Bible. I didn't have one. I asked one of the officers for one as she was walking past me with several in her hands, but her response was a strong "No. Fill out the proper paperwork if you want one!"

Putting in a request through the proper paperwork meant I would have to wait several days to be granted a

Bible. I was hungry for His Word now, so I asked God to give me a Bible if He wanted me to have one.

When I awoke the next morning, there was a Bible lying on the little table in my cell. I tapped on my cellmate's bunk above me and asked if he knew where it had come from. My cellmate wasn't a Christian and had no interest in God whatsoever. He couldn't even read very well. But as he had been walking to our cell before lockdown time the previous night, he'd seen one of the jail officers with a Bible in his hands. For no reason he could explain, he'd felt led to ask if he could have it. The officer had given it to him. Now, he told me, he didn't really even want it and I could have it if I wanted it. I thanked God for giving me a Bible.

Lockdown time lasted twenty-four hours, so I spent it with the Word of God. At the end of that lockdown time, the guards came for me and told me to get dressed because I had an appointment with a doctor in town. I was surprised because I hadn't asked to see the doctor, but somehow an appointment had been scheduled for me. They shackled my hands and feet and took me in the back of a police car to the doctor's office.

There, the doctor examined me and asked why I was taking all of the medications I was on. He could tell they were affecting my mind. I explained to him that I had made a mistake by telling the other doctors I was hearing voices when I really wasn't. He signed orders to immediately take me off the medications and to give me something to help detox my body. God worked this miracle to get my mind free of the medicines.

As my mind began to get clear from all the drugs, one of the inmates in jail told me about a lawyer he knew who could help me. I called my grandfather and then he called my father to ask him to go see the lawyer. Before long I had a probation bond set for me. My father signed the bond and soon I was out of jail.

The next day, I thought it was best to go tell my probation officer where I was. Several weeks earlier he had visited me in jail and had told me he'd put me there for my own good. He'd been certain that there was no way I was going to get a bond to get out of jail before my hearing with the judge.

I went to Guerry Phillips' office and asked the secretary to tell Guerry that David Piper was there to see him. She picked up the phone and told him. I could hear reaction of his disbelief over the phone receiver. "What?! Are you sure he said David Piper? It can't be! Tell him not to move!" In what seemed like less than a second, Guerry was in front of me. He couldn't believe he was seeing me outside of jail.

"Follow me," he ordered, and we went down the hall to his office. After we were seated, he asked, "How did you do it?"

I said, "Prayer changes things."

"No, David. I asked you how you did it. How'd you get bond?"

Again, I said, "Prayer changes things." I could see the frustration on his face, and I knew he was convinced that I was so self-destructive that I'd never survive on the outside. I told him the sequence of events that had brought me into his office, including all of the miracles God had done.

After hearing my story, Guerry told me how sorry he was for having to put me in jail and he asked me to forgive him. He told me to stay straight and he would see me at the probation hearing. We both knew I was facing a possible thirty-year prison sentence. I needed another miracle.

In the days that followed that meeting with Guerry, I found a church, met with the pastor, and became accountable to him. He put me into a good discipleship program in one of the church's small groups, and I even joined the church softball team. Life seemed to be turning around for me for the first time. I was beginning to get a good foothold on that path of obedience and was slowly starting upward into a whole new life.

When the time came for the probation hearing, I stood before the judge and the favor of God fell on me. The judge asked my probation officer for his opinion on what the court should do with me. Guerry responded by telling him I had been a model probationer and that I had always done what he'd asked during my probation. I couldn't believe my ears when I heard the judge dismiss the charges and release me. I stood in amazement.

Once again, God's mercy that never ends had overshadowed my life. I was beginning to understand that God had a call on my life, but there was something required of me: obedience and the responsibility to stay in His Word.

I'd learned so much. I'd learned that God will discipline me to train me and keep me on the right path. I also found out that the Christian life wasn't meant to be walked alone, that we need others to come alongside us, people to hold us accountable, to help us stay on the path of obedience.

Finding mentors and accountability partners is so important because we have an enemy who lays traps for us, seeking to draw us away from God and off the path. God's Word says that Satan is like a roaring lion looking for someone he can devour (see 1 Peter 5:8). To keep from being swallowed up by the enemy, we all need someone to guard our backs. When we start getting that Lone Ranger mentality, that it's-just-me-and-God-against-the-world attitude, we isolate ourselves, and that puts us in a vulnerable position to become prey for the devil. And make no mistake about it, he will attack you if you are isolated.

If you're playing the Lone Ranger Christian, it's only a matter of time before the enemy drags you back down to the bottom. If you want to stay right with God and you want to receive all that He has for you, then get involved in a local body of believers, get a mentor, get accountability partners. You need people who will tell you things about yourself that you won't like to hear— people who will tell you the truth about yourself. These are the people who will hold up a mirror for you to see if there is stuff in your life that is unpleasant and shouldn't be there. The only way you can see this stuff is if God puts somebody in your life to tell you about it.

When we leave the path of disobedience and make it around the U-turn onto the path of obedience, God expects us to change. Why? Because it's the only way to stay on the path that leads to that fuller life He's promised us! Included in that change process is coming into the knowledge that a successful life can only be gained by a group effort.

Have you ever seen a kindergarten class on a field trip? Did you notice that the teacher and the parents always make all of the kids hold hands as they walk from place to place? This is so that no one gets lost or hurt or snatched away by a stranger.

As God's kids, God expects us all to hold hands as we travel along on this journey we call the Christian life. And it's for the very same reasons that the kindergarten teacher makes all her kids walk together: so we don't get lost or hurt or snatched away by a "stranger" and so that we have plenty of people around us to pick us up when we fall.

The Bible describes God's pathway through life as "straight and narrow," but it's also rocky. If you don't watch your footing and travel with a partner, it's far too easy to stumble, and you don't want to fall if you have no one alongside to help pick you up again.

CHAPTER FIVE

DEFENDING YOUR WEAK PLACES

When tempted, no one should say, "God is tempting me." For God cannot be tempted by evil, nor does he tempt anyone; but each one is tempted when, by his own evil desire, he is dragged away and enticed.

James 1:13-14

There is a war over every soul who is close to coming to Christ or who has made a commitment to Christ but who is not yet equipped to do battle with the enemy. Satan is not interested in taking down unbelievers—he's already got them where he wants them; and he knows he can't take down believers who know who they are in Christ and are walking in the power of the Holy Spirit. His battle plan is to prevent those who are seeking God from finding Him, and to take down new, young believers before they become mighty warriors for the Kingdom. He wants to keep the numbers in God's army small.

Satan's battle plan is dependent on knowing your weaknesses and using them against you. This is why it is so imperative that you know your own weaknesses—so you can guard against his attacks.

We all have our own unique weaknesses. Some of us are bound by fear of rejection. Some of us struggle with anger. Some of us are trapped in an unforgiving attitude. Others are ensnared in addictions. Regardless of what your particular weakness is, the first line of defense is to avoid putting yourself in situations that make you vulnerable to the attacks of the enemy.

Are you an alcoholic? Stay away from bars and drinking parties. Are you a drug addict? Stay away from people who are still using. Are you a codependent? Stay out of unhealthy relationships. Do you have an uncontrollable temper? Stay away from people and situations that set you off. Is any of this easy? No! Defending your weak place is an everyday struggle. The apostle Paul warns us in Ephesians, "Do not give the devil a foothold" (Ephesians 4:27).

Our second line of defense is to make sure we are not walking alone. I can't repeat it often enough that we all need other, more mature Christians around us to help us protect our backs (and I want to stress the words "more mature"). When your back is exposed to the devil, you are vulnerable to an attack against your weak place.

When a lion attacks a flock of sheep, he doesn't drive into the middle of the herd and pick out the biggest ram. He first looks for a sheep that has isolated itself. If he can't find one, then he'll try to separate a sheep from the herd, preferably one that is on the fringes of the flock, and better, one with its back exposed so he can pounce on it.

If you're on the fringe of God's "flock" and your back is exposed, be aware that there is a "lion" stalking you!

So, do we blame the devil when our lives get messed up? No! The devil is only doing what he's always done—looking for victims. If you've become a victim, is it because you've taken the position and posture of a victim? Have you isolated yourself where the enemy can reach you? If you've allied yourself with other believers, if you've made yourself accountable to a mentor who is more mature in Christ than you are, and if you've identified your weaknesses, then you've taken the necessary precautions needed to keep from being exposed to the enemy. After you do all of this, if you still find yourself out there where you can be attacked and dragged back into disobedience, then it's most likely because you're playing with temptation instead of fleeing from it. Don't slow dance with the devil if you don't want to get burned!

This is not only imperative for us, it's also crucial for everyone around us whom we love and who loves us. Falling into temptation, and consequently into disobedience, causes hurt to our families, our friends and others in our lives who may be weaker than we are. We can become a stumbling block to others, tripping them up in their faith also.

I know what it is to fall into temptation. I can teach these things from experience. In the time that followed my decision to live for God, I was still living on the fringes of the "flock." Even though I had gotten involved in a good church and was in a discipleship program, I had foolishly left my back exposed.

The softball team I had joined at my new church had a few players on it who saw nothing wrong with being a Christian and drinking beer, but for someone like me who was a recovering alcoholic, being around these guys was playing with temptation. I played right into the hands of the enemy. A few sips turned into a few slips that turned into a major fall in my life. Not only did I start drinking again, and using again, but this time my disobedience hurt the people I loved the most — my family.

After my surrender to the Lord and my latest experience behind bars, I had reconciled with my uncle, aunt and cousins, family members I had lived with for a time as a kid. They had been so pleased with what God had done in my life that they had helped me get established in church and in the discipleship program. My next fall into disobedience caused me to betray their trust in me. In order to pay for my habits, I began stealing from these wonderful people who had given me so much.

This time the conviction of the Holy Spirit was very strong on me. I hated myself so much for what I was doing that I drove out of town with the intention of finding somewhere to kill myself. When I was about one hundred eighty miles out of town, I ran into my cousin at a convenience store. I told him that I wanted to die and why. He then told me his story, which was worse than mine, and said that he didn't want to kill himself. I figured that if he didn't want to die, and his life was worse, then I didn't really want to die either.

The next day, I turned around and drove back home. When I arrived, I was arrested by the police. They had warrants against me for burglary and forgery.

What I didn't know then was that God was allowing every bit of this to happen for good, and not just for my good but also for the good of those people whose lives I would touch inside the walls of jail and prison. The trouble I was about to face would be a testing and training ground that would teach me many things about faith and obedience, and it would open doors for me to share the love of Jesus with many others.

All of this happened in November 1997, just a short time before Christmas. I was incarcerated to await arraignment on the charges. I was still on thirty years' probation from the last time I had broken the law, and now I would be facing the possibility that my probation would be revoked and on top of that being sentenced for the new charges.

When I stood before the judge in December, I was sentenced to twenty-one months in the Georgia Department of Corrections Detention Center for my latest mistakes and facing a much longer term for having broken probation. I now belonged to the State of Georgia. Although I was being held at the county jail, I would soon be taken from there and sent to the State of Georgia's facility for incarceration.

The hardest part of all of this was knowing I was inflicting hurt and embarrassment on my family, especially on my daughter. Megan was now facing Christmas with her father in prison.

I knew I had messed up again and was immediately repentant. I didn't have the strength to overcome my addictions on my own. I had already tried every treatment center, mental hospital program and twelve-step program available to me. Man's programs could only bring the addictions under control temporarily. I knew that I could only be truly set free by God, because only God could cure me completely.

I began to seek the Lord immediately during my incarceration, and with my decision to do so came a new level of persecution from inside the jail.

There is a world all its own inside the jailhouse walls. In that world there is a term the officers use for Christianity among the inmates—it's called jailhouse religion. The reason for that is because so many offenders seem to keep going through a revolving door into and out of jail. When they are locked up, they grab their Bibles and start praying, but when they're released, they leave their Bibles and their faith behind while they return to the same life outside that they had before.

Seeing so many offenders go through this revolving door into and out of the prison system made the law enforcement officers doubtful that any offender could ever really change. It also caused them to look upon a prisoner's faith in God through cynical eyes. When that so-called faith seemed to disappear the moment the prisoner was released, how could it be sincere? This line of thinking would often lead to the mocking of an offender's faith.

Through my life, God was going to show the officers in the county jail and the prison that there really was a way for someone to leave a life of incarceration and change to a whole new way of living. He was going to make a living example of me in order to do this.

That December, all I could think about was how much I had hurt my family and that my daughter would be spending Christmas without her father. To be honest, I knew I had not been a very good father up to that point. I had shown her little love and support due to the condition in which I'd lived most of my life, but that didn't change the fact that I loved her with all my heart. I knew I desperately needed healing from my addictions so that I could be the daddy she'd never had.

I called Megan, my daughter, around the third week of December to ask if she wanted me to come home for Christmas. Her reply was, "Of course I do." So I told her that she would need to start praying and asking the Holy Spirit to help her pray to ask God if He would please send me home for Christmas.

I then called my dad and asked him if he would ask the Holy Spirit to help him pray for me to be released to come home for Christmas. My father told me it was impossible, that I had been sentenced and I now belonged to the State of Georgia. He was angry with me and said, "You did the crime; now do the time."

I told him to get his Bible and read Luke 1:37. Then I hung up, trusting the Lord to work in my father.

After I had hung up, my dad went to his Bible and opened it to Luke 1:37, which read, *"For nothing is impossible with God."* My dad's faith level began to rise. He asked the Holy Spirit to help him pray, and he prayed asking God to send his boy home for Christmas. Then he did a very bold thing. He got up, went to the phone, and called the judge who'd sentenced me, asking him to please let his son come home for Christmas. The line was quiet for about thirty seconds, and then a miracle happened. The judge said, "Yes, I will send your boy home for Christmas." God had spoken to the judge's heart.

The judge kept his word. He did the paperwork and set into motion everything that needed to happen to release me long enough to spend Christmas with my family. My daughter, my father, and I had all prayed in faith and God had answered. The sheriff told us that he had never seen this judge do something like this and that he was really going out on a limb by doing so. But God did the miracle in the judge and I was able to spend a day and a half on furlough over Christmas with my daughter and family.

After I went back to jail, I was placed in an area for protective custody. My former cellmate was jealous that I had been released for Christmas and was convinced that I had snitched on someone to get the privilege, so he had threatened to kill me. This inmate was known to throw water on the preacher during the inmates' "church night." For my own protection, they kept me away from this man.

When I was finally placed safely back in the main area of the county jail, I was placed in a section where the "weekenders" (offenders who were incarcerated during weekends to do time for short-term sentences) were placed and where the people needing special care were housed.

As I walked into that cell block, I felt an unusual atmosphere unlike the regular jail environment—it was a strong presence of the Lord. In this cell block was a seventy-one-year-old man named Robert Lowther, but everyone called him "Pop." He only came out of his cell to take a shower, get his medications and eat. This day he came up to me and said, "You can have my food. I am not eating." The other inmates told me that he had not been eating for weeks.

When I asked Pop why he hadn't been eating, he told me that he was fasting and praying. He had once been a preacher, but had walked away from the call of God on his life and had gone into a life of sin. He believed that the Lord had allowed his present circumstances to discipline him.

During the time I was in this block waiting transfer to the State's incarceration facility, Pop would become a considerable influence in my life. One of the first things he did was tell me that God had given him a word of knowledge for me. He said God was going to take my spirit to a place where the Lord Himself would speak with me concerning my future. He told me to keep a pen and paper by my bedside because I would need to write down whatever the Lord told me.

That very night it happened. I was awakened out of deep sleep by a sound and suddenly found myself flying over some mountains to the most beautiful place I'd ever seen. The feeling I had was indescribable. And then, God's voice came to me, still and small, but at the same time loud and clear. He spoke to me about the great things ahead that He had planned for my life. The visitation lasted what seemed to be a brief moment, and then I was suddenly back in my bunk in the jail cell. I was electrified and overcome with emotions of happiness, but then I remembered that I still had a jail sentence to finish out. I looked down at the pad of paper I had placed at my bedside and saw these words: "Call unto Me and I will answer you and show you great and mighty things planned for your life that you do not yet know."

The days and months that followed this event would be filled with many miracles inside the walls of the Worth County Jail and the State of Georgia Detention Center.

CHAPTER SIX

BECOMING USEFUL TO GOD

I appeal to you for my son Onesimus, who became my son while I was in chains. Formerly he was useless to you, but now he has become useful both to you and to me.   Philemon 10-11

In his letter to Philemon at Colosse, the apostle Paul pleaded for mercy on behalf of Onesimus. You see, Onesimus had been a slave in Philemon's household. He had stolen money from his master and then had run away to Rome.

While in Rome, Onesimus met Paul and became a Christian. Onesimus had left a life of disobedience, and Paul was now mentoring him on how to walk in obedience to the Lord. The runaway slave was now working with Paul in ministering the Gospel.

Soon Paul would be sending Onesimus back to Philemon's household, the place where he was known as a thief, so Paul wrote a letter to Philemon to let him know of the change in his runaway slave's life. While Onesimus had been "useless" before, God had worked such a miraculous change in his life that he was now considered by the apostle Paul to be *"useful."*

This is the same thing that God wants to work in every believer's life. When we're living in disobedience, we're living a life of uselessness. There is no eternal value in anything that we do. But once we become children of God, the Lord begins to train us through Christian mentors and through circumstances in order to make us useful to Him. The training process may take a while, and there may be many failures among the successes, but as long as we're willing to submit to that training process, God will use us for His glory and continue to shape us into useful servants for the Gospel of Jesus Christ.

This is where I was in my life while I was living in that county jail. Pop had become the "Paul" in my life. I watched God use him among the other prisoners, and I learned, and I started to become useful to the Lord.

God began to bless and protect Pop and me in the county jail. We ministered to the other inmates, and as those weekenders would accept Jesus and be touched by the presence of God, they would carry that back out of the jail to their families and friends. The Lord was really using Pop's life and showing me an example in him that I could follow.

One day Pop told me that God was about to touch me in a new way. He told me to raise my hands up. I did, and when Pop laid his hands on my hands, the power of God fell over me. I broke out in uncontrollable laughter for eight solid hours. The other inmates thought I had flipped out. I was glad there were no cameras in that cell block, or the jailhouse officials surely would have shipped me to isolation.

There were times when God's presence was so strong in the place that it seemed there had to be an angel sitting on top of the building. Sometimes at night, Pop would wake up and begin to sing "How Great Thou Art," and the glory of God would begin to manifest right there, stronger than I've seen it in some churches. God was filling me with His joy and His anointing for my next ministry opportunity. He was planning to make me useful in ministering His Gospel.

One day I was waiting in my cell for the officers to let us out to shower when I was informed that I was going to be transferred to a neighboring county to face more charges against me. I wasn't to come back to this jail. The sheriff had left word with the neighboring county officials that I had answered all the charges in his county and that they could keep me over there until my transfer came through to the state prison. They came for me early that same day to take me there.

The deputy who came to pick me up was a born again, Spirit-filled believer. In fact, every person assigned to guard me that day was born again.

On the way to the jail in the other county, the Holy Spirit fell on us in the car and the deputy driving the car began to prophesy over my life about what God would do through me. We finally arrived at the other jail, and when he went to take the handcuffs off me, the power of God came off me and hit him. He began to shake all over and could hardly do his job because he was shaking so hard.

When he took my mug shot, he said he saw a halo over me through the camera lens and could not take his eyes off me. But then he put me in a safe place. He seemed worried about my safety there, and kept an eye on me the whole time I was there.

The jail in the other county was old and very overcrowded. They were in the process of building a new one, but the facility they had at that time was very dark and musty. It reminded me of the belly of a fish. I know now that God was letting me see just how bad it could get. The jail I had just left had been clean and neat, almost like the jail in Mayberry on *The Andy Griffith Show*. We'd had a considerable amount of freedom considering we were prisoners. But this jail was much different. The smell was horrendous, and people were practically sleeping on top of one another.

The Lord spoke to me and told me not to talk to or look at anyone while I was there. I was also not to let any of the other inmates lay hands on me unless the Lord told me to. So, for hours, I would not speak to or look anyone in the eye. Hours went by. Then they put me into the general population. I can't begin to describe the conditions in that jail. It seemed like hell on earth. The smell, the environment, the overcrowding—it all seemed more than any man could stand.

After several hours in there, I was taken to be interviewed by the detective working on my case. It turned out that he was also a born again, Spirit-filled believer. As we talked, he told me that he could feel the glory of God on my life and that he was going to help me. He said he didn't know why, but he just could not keep me in this place. The charges against me in this county could be run concurrently with my other sentences so no additional time would be added to my jail time. The detective was going to send me back to the prison I had just left. He sent me back to the cell to wait. This was God's favor working in my life.

I waited in the cell with all those other guys. There were two young men sleeping on the floor. I heard the Lord tell me to talk to these two, and when they woke up, one of them said to me, "Hey, mister, do you have a Bible?" I told them I did. He asked if my Bible looked like his, and he showed me a little New Testament. I told him that I had a big Bible with both the Old and New Testaments in it. The young guy told me that he was having trouble understanding the scriptures and didn't know how to be saved. He asked if I would tell him how he could be saved.

The Lord told me that once I had led these two men to Him the officers would come for me and transfer me back to the safety of the other jail.

I began to explain everything I knew about God's plan of salvation in Jesus and how they could accept Jesus into their hearts. Those two boys began to cry, and as soon as they were done praying to receive Jesus, a voice down the hall called my name. It was the guard coming to take me back to the other county jail. God kept His word and did a miracle to get me back into the jail where Pop was.

Back where I had started, God continued to use me in powerful ways, but after almost two months in the county jail, it finally came time for "Pop" and me to go our separate ways: Pop was sent to the Men's State Prison in north Georgia, where he still is today, and I was sent to the State of Georgia Detention Center. I had already spent several months in the prison system, and I had gotten to a place where I was ready to obey Him in anything He would ask me to do. Every night before going to bed I would spend time on my face by my bunk asking Him to bless my family and my enemies.

In response to my prayers and my obedience, I saw the Lord do literal miracles. One day I was in the bathroom praising God, and another prisoner, a young man I'll call "Kenny," approached me wanting to know how I could be so happy when I was locked up in prison. Kenny was deaf in one ear. I explained to him that I had

Jesus in my life, but even more importantly, I had the Person of the Holy Spirit living inside of me, giving me the ability to praise God in spite of my circumstances.

Kenny was a Jehovah's Witness and didn't understand what I was talking about, but the Holy Spirit continued to draw this young man to me. As he witnessed the joy in my life, he saw something inside of me that he wanted in his own life. I began to minister to him about the Person of the Holy Spirit, and after leading him to Jesus, I told him how to talk to the Holy Spirit.

The next day Kenny came running to me, excited and shouting, "I got it! I got it!" He was feeling the joy of the Lord. I told him what he had was Jesus. He was so happy that he wanted more. I told him that the Holy Spirit would make Himself real in his life if he would just pray and ask the Spirit to become manifest in his life. He began to pray every day for the Holy Spirit to become more tangible to him.

One day as I was listening to a Christian radio station over my the headphones on my Walkman, Kenny was talking to me and bubbling over. He talked and talked about the Lord, and I began to get annoyed because I couldn't hear the music. The Lord immediately rebuked me, and told me, "Listen to him. He's hungry for more of Me." I switched off the radio and began to listen to this new babe in Christ talk about the Lord.

All of a sudden, the power of God came on me as we were talking about the Holy Spirit. I knew that a healing anointing had just come upon me. I told Kenny that the power of God had just showed up on my life to heal the sick. He revealed to me then that he had been deaf in his left ear since the day of his birth. His mother had tried to abort him with pills when he was in the womb.

Even though God had saved his life, he was unable to hear in his left ear.

I told him that the same Jesus who had saved him was also able to heal him. I prayed for his ear right there on the spot, and the power of God opened that boy's ear. For the first time in his life he was able to hear out of his left ear.

News of this miracle spread throughout the cell block, and eventually to the officials. They made arrangements for Kenny to be shipped off to another facility miles away. They were fearful that I might have some sort of mind control over Kenny, like some kind of cult leader. They just didn't understand that it was the Lord who was really in control of both of us.

The head official we called "Pharaoh," heard about it too and didn't like it, because he had grown not to like me very much. I had apparently gotten on his bad side over my work with the prison library.

The local Christian radio station had sent me a program guide with listings of ministries that had broadcasts over their station. One day the Holy Spirit had directed me to write to some of those ministries to request book donations for the prison library. It was in very bad shape. There was very little Christian reading material but there was a great deal of occult and New Age material.

Soon after writing, we began to receive boxes and boxes of brand new books, all centered on Christ, which were being sent into this head official's office. This created tension between us. He got angry at the amount of Christian material overloading his office and told me he didn't want to see any more of it. He apparently despised everything to do with religion. Then he put me in charge of the library to stock the new books to get them out of his office. I spent several days replacing the demonic materials with the Christian books.

After hearing about Kenny's healing, "Pharaoh" came to me, asking, "What's this I hear about you praying for that boy and healing him?"

I told him that I hadn't healed Kenny, that Jesus had. "Pharaoh" was not saved and didn't like me or trust me, so he didn't understand and didn't want to.

In spite of the opinion of some of the officials, God continued to use me inside the prison. Over time as I shared Jesus with the other inmates, I watched as the Holy Spirit would draw broken hearts to Jesus and one young man after another would ask Jesus to be his Savior. These were not just "jailhouse conversions"; they were sincere conversions for Christ.

At night, right before bedtime, many of these new converts would form healing lines at my bunk. They would line up on the right and the left, asking for prayer. The hunger for a touch from God on their lives was starting to spread to inmates throughout the entire prison dorm.

God was decidedly moving through me, but the work that He was doing didn't come unopposed by the enemy. Satan did try to come against me in the prison, but when he did, God showed Himself strong on my behalf by providing me with protection. The Lord took the wildest, craziest inmate in my prison dorm, changed his life around, and turned him into my bodyguard. His story is another miracle of God.

I was dressing to go out into the yard for exercise one day, putting on layer after layer of clothing because it was cold outside, when I noticed this crazy inmate lying on his bunk. This fellow I'll refer to as "Nick", was known to be unpredictable. No one ever knew when he would go nuts and start a fight. He didn't like white people, and spent a lot of time in solitary confinement because of the fighting. As I was dressing, the Lord told me to go pray for Nick.

Silently I told the Lord that I really didn't want to go pray for him. I was afraid of what he'd do to me. As I was debating the situation with the Lord, Nick got up and went to the bathroom. I sensed an opportunity, so I hurried over, laid my hands on his empty bunk and said, "Lord Jesus, anoint this bed to change this man."

Immediately the Holy Spirit rebuked me, saying, "That is not what I told you to do. I said you are to pray for this man, not his empty bed."

Nick came back and crawled back into his bunk, pulling his blanket up to his chin. I remembered the rumor that Nick was in prison because he had shot up his own mother's house. Slowly, I gathered up my courage and told the Lord, "Okay, Lord. I'll do what You ask, but You'll have to protect me."

I went and stood over Nick as he lay in his bunk. He seemed as though he wasn't well. He looked up at me with those crazy eyes, and I said, "Is something wrong with you?" I didn't know at the time that he was in intense pain from a tooth problem. His mouth was swollen with infection and his gum was bleeding.

He didn't answer me, just shook his head in the affirmative and pointed to his mouth. I asked if I could pray for him. Nick nodded his head to say "yes." I reached down and simply touched the side of his face, saying, "In the name of Jesus, devil, come out of him!" He sat up in his bed with a wild look, just staring at me. I felt something happen and just smiled. I didn't need to wait—I knew God had healed the man. I left him there and went outside, thanking the Lord the whole way.

When I went back inside an hour later, I heard that Nick had jumped up and run to the bathroom to look inside his mouth. His pain had stopped instantly when I'd prayed for him, and in the bathroom mirror, he had seen that the bleeding had stopped and the swelling had disappeared. Others told me Nick had gone back to his bunk to stand on it and scream, "It's real! It's real! God really did it!" He told everybody around him that he'd seen miracles on TV before, but had never really believed in them.

After that, Nick and I became friends. He became my personal bodyguard at his own choosing. He warned everyone they had better be nice to me or they would answer to him. Even the officers told me they would never have believed it if it hadn't happened to the meanest, craziest inmate they had ever seen.

The problem was that the change in Nick didn't last. Two weeks later, he became meaner and crazier than ever. The officers came to me and asked me to do something to help since Nick was now my friend. I told them I would ask the Lord what had happened.

I prayed and sought the Lord, not realizing at the time that this would be a training exercise for a future in full-time ministry. The Lord told me that He had performed the miracle for Nick to bring him to salvation, but I had not led Nick to Jesus. Healing is a great miracle, but salvation is the greatest miracle and I had forgotten to lead Nick into salvation, so the devil that had left Nick had returned with others.

The Word of God says in Matthew 12:

"When an evil spirit comes out of a man, it goes through arid places seeking rest and does not find it.

Then it says, 'I will return to the house I left.' When it arrives, it finds the house unoccupied, swept clean and put in order. Then it goes and takes with it seven other spirits more wicked than itself, and they go in and live there. And the final condition of that man is worse than the first. That is how it will be with this wicked generation." Matthew 12:43-45

I read this passage to the officers. They told me to fix the problem, so the next day when I saw Nick in the bathroom, I asked him what was wrong with him. He told me that he had a terrible headache this time. I asked if I could pray for him and once again he agreed. Again, I ordered the devil in him to come out in the name of Jesus.

His face looked happy and surprised. "It's gone! It's gone!" This time, I didn't make the same mistake. I immediately began to tell him about Jesus and what He had died for on the cross. The Holy Spirit convicted him and he accepted Jesus as his Savior. From that time forward, Nick was a changed man. He would always be in church services and could be found reading his Bible.

Soon I learned that my time in prison would end much earlier than I had imagined. After only eight months of serving my sentence, God began to put together all the pieces necessary to get me out of prison early. I had received a little book called *Prison to Praise*, by Merlin Caruthers, that taught all of us how to praise God no matter what our circumstances. As I began to use the power of prayer and praise, God began to give me favor with the judge.

The judge had originally sentenced me to twenty-one months, which was to include time in the detention center as well as in a halfway house where I was to work and remain until my fine was paid. Now he decided, in spite of the probation people, that it was time for me to be released to live in the halfway house and get a job to support myself, but God had other plans. I had shown myself to be humble and broken over my mistakes and over my disobedience to Him, and so His mercy flowed into my life. My grandfather had gone to see the judge to ask him about releasing me early. I believe that God must have spoken to the judge, because he had agreed to my early release.

Eight months after the day I entered prison for a twenty-one month sentence, I was set free once again. Within the next year and a half after my release, God would intervene in such a way that I would be taken completely off all probation and given my rights back as a citizen. Only the mercy and power of God could have brought about these miracles.

CHAPTER SEVEN

THE CRY OF DESPERATION

Listen to my cry, for I am in desperate need.... Set me free from my prison, that I may praise your name.

Psalm 142:6-7

The scene is the lakeside of the Sea of Galilee. Jesus and His disciples have just returned from a trip to the other side of the lake, and a large crowd is gathering around Him. The woman watches and waits for her opportunity. She knows she may have only one chance and that there could be serious consequences if she fails. She knows that He is her last hope.

There are crowds of people all around Him, but He moves easily through them as they part for Him to move among them. Now she sees that He is moving toward her. Her heart begins to beat wildly in fear and excitement. She is hoping and praying that He will come close enough.

But suddenly He turns and starts moving in another direction. Panic rises in her heart. *No! Please come back!* She begins to push her way through the crowd. She is desperate in her desire to be free from her curse.

The crowd is thick, so she pushes, pulls and pries her

way toward Him. Then, just as she is close enough to reach out and touch Him, He starts to move away again. She makes a desperate grab and manages to catch only the hem of His cloak. Suddenly she can feel the power of God coursing through her body like a flood. She catches her breath in astonishment. The bleeding she has endured for twelve years has suddenly stopped.

"Who touched Me?" Jesus' voice rings above the crowd. He has stopped to look around for the one who has received what was not given. "Who touched My clothes?"

Some begin to turn to her, having seen her frantic grab. She meets His eyes, knowing that He knows. She is afraid. In fear of His wrath, she throws herself at His feet, confessing the truth. Yes, she was the one who touched Him because she knew He had the power to heal her.

"Daughter," He calls her. She looks up into His eyes. There is no anger in them—there is only compassion. "Your faith has healed you. Go in peace and be freed from your suffering."

The gospels in the New Testament contain some powerful stories of people who desperately needed Jesus to touch them. You can read about the woman with the issue of blood in Mark 5:25-34. She was only one of many people described in the gospels who had reached a point of desperation.

This woman had been living with an unbearable condition. She had been bleeding for twelve years. In the Jewish culture of the day, this made her unclean, and according to Jewish law, if a person touches someone who is unclean, that person also becomes unclean.

But she had been following Jesus' ministry and had seen His miracles of healing. She had heard His words and had received a new hope, and this new hope had stirred up inside of her a desperation to receive the promises of God. She became desperate to receive healing, desperate to receive something more out of life than merely existing. Because of her desire to be set free and her desperation to reach Jesus, she received what she needed from Him.

Many of us are like this woman. We've heard His Words and His promises. Hope has been stirred in our hearts, but we're still bound by curses that plague us and that keep us from fully following Him. We reach a point of desperation to be set free.

Friend, if this is you, then know that Jesus is ready and willing to set you free. You just need to be desperate enough to pursue Him and to surrender to Him so you can receive your freedom. He's not angry with you for your failures—His compassion is endless. He's ready and willing to give you the freedom you need *as soon as you are ready to walk in obedience to Him.*

I can write about these things from experience. I know what it's like to continue to fail. I know what it's like to reach the point of desperation. Even after the amazing things God had done in me and through me up to this point in my life, and even after the miracles I had received in getting my early release from prison, I was still bound by my addictions. I desperately wanted to be free from them.

I heard about an upcoming Benny Hinn crusade in Birmingham, Alabama, and I was determined to go. I had been to a previous crusade several years before in 1994 in Atlanta with my grandmother, my grandfather and my father. They had asked me to drive them there, and though I had agreed only so I could do the party scene in that city, I had ended up sitting through the crusade long enough to feel the power of God touch me briefly. I had never forgotten that day.

Later, while in the county jail, I had watched *This Is Your Day*, which was (and still is) Benny Hinn's television program. Many of the inmates watched, and we would sit and cry as the anointing of God came right through the TV set. We were totally in awe of the miracles that God did through Benny Hinn's ministry.

I had marked my calendar with his crusade schedule, and when my release from prison finally came, I was determined to attend at least one of them. My hope was that I would find freedom from my addictions at one of his crusades. My faith in God was strong at this point, and I believed God would use Benny Hinn to help me just as He had done for so many others.

Now Pastor Benny was going to be in Birmingham. Just released from prison, I managed to land a good job right away in sales, but I informed my boss when he hired me that I would need September 16 and 17 off in order to take a trip to a church meeting in Birmingham. He told me that if I worked hard and did my job, he had no problem with my taking those days off, so I started work, anticipating those dates in September when I could go to Birmingham.

It was July when I was released. There were two and a half months until the crusade. That amount of time with no help turned out to be my downfall once again. I wanted Jesus to rule in my life, but now that I was out where I could easily get drugs and alcohol, my flesh overpowered my spirit and I began using again. This episode with drugs was particularly vicious, yet in spite of that I managed to do my job and outsold many of the other salesmen.

When September 16 and 17 came close, I went to my boss and reminded him that I needed those two days off. He flatly refused to give me those dates off work. Because the crusade was in another state and because I needed to maintain my job to keep my probation, I went to my probation officer with my problem.

God had given me another Christian probation officer just like Guerry Phillips. This man was willing to listen to my problem and he was sympathetic. Unlike some other probation officers who would send you back to prison in a heartbeat, he wanted to see me get better, so he gave me permission to go to the crusade. With his knowledge, I quit my job, got into my car and headed for Alabama.

Birmingham was 350 miles away. I knew no one there and I had very little money in my pocket, but I went anyway, looking for freedom from my addictions. I arrived the night before the crusade and managed to find a budget motel room that I could afford. Though I had come all this way, I hadn't left my desire for drugs behind. That desire started pulling at me. I was weak and gave in to it. I left the motel to find a neighborhood that looked like a good place to find drugs.

Finally, around 2:00 AM, I spotted a bar. Inside, the people were all dressed in black. Some had spiked hair and others had purple hair. I definitely looked out of place. This was not the night scene I was used to, but it did look like the right place to find some dope.

When I walked up to the bar, they could tell right away by looking at me that I was from out of town. A man and woman sitting at the bar asked me where I was from. I told them I had come to town from Georgia for the Benny Hinn crusade. They asked if Benny Hinn was the man in the white suit who had all the miracles in his services. I told them yes, that was him, but the miracles weren't about Benny, they were about Jesus.

When I mentioned the name of Jesus, the woman jumped up, grabbed her purse and said, "I can't take this any more." She began shouting and then ran out of the bar.

The man, left sitting at the bar alone, said, "Thanks a lot, buddy. You just blew my chance to have the evening of a lifetime."

It turned out that the lady was married and had met this man at the bar for the first time that night to have an affair with him. God had just used me to accomplish His will even though I had come in there for all the wrong reasons. I was so shocked by all of this that a holy fear and reverence for God came over me. I left without ever getting any drugs. I went back to my motel room and went to sleep instead.

Not only had God intervened in that lady's life, but He had also intervened in mine. He had rescued me from destroying my chance to find the freedom I so desperately needed.

The next day, I arrived at the civic center around 2:00 in the afternoon. Crowds of people had already arrived and the lines had already begun to form. There were many people standing in line who were in need of a miracle, just like me. Some were afflicted with sicknesses; other were battling life-threatening diseases; yet there was an air of expectancy among them. Though the service was still five hours away, songs of praise and worship were being lifted up from all of the lines.

I worked my way around the civic center and got into the shortest line. The whole time I was still fighting the desire to go find drugs. The people around me freely shared their stories of why they had come, so I did the same. Some of us prayed together. I made some special friends that day, and some of them I have kept in contact with even to this day.

That night as the service began, the power of God filled the arena. High praises of worship to the Creator rose to the ceilings. The atmosphere was electric. It felt as if God Himself had left His throne to come sit among us to enjoy the worship.

Later, during the service, Pastor Benny called for people who felt they were being healed to step out of their seats and come down front to give their testimonies. I stepped out of my seat in faith, believing that I had been touched by God's healing power, and I made my way down toward the front of the arena to tell someone.

The lines were almost half a football field away from the platform and I was stuck at the back of one. I couldn't get anywhere near the stage. Knowing I'd never get to the front of the line by the end of the service, I prayed and asked the Lord for a miracle to get me up to the front if He really wanted me to be prayed for by Pastor Benny.

About five minutes after that prayer, a volunteer member of Pastor Benny's staff came straight past everyone right to me like an arrow. His name was Rusty, and he asked me what God was doing for me. I told him my situation. Rusty told me to follow him. He took me right through the crowd toward the front. It looked like the Red Sea parting before us as we made our way to the front platform. Within minutes, I was standing up on that platform in front of Benny Hinn.

Pastor Benny asked me what work God was doing in me, what was happening. I explained how I had quit my job and driven 350 miles to be there because I was desperate to be delivered from drug addictions, from the influence of witchcraft, and from the demons that had been haunting me. Pastor Benny then prayed for me.

I left the platform. Before I could leave, the ministry had me sign a release form giving them permission to follow up on me. This permission would give them access to my medical records, my criminal records, and all the other documentation in my life in order to verify that a miracle had really taken place in my life.

Afterward, I returned to my motel room, excited by how God had made a way for me to be prayed for by Benny Hinn, who had such a strong anointing on his life. That night, as I got ready for bed, I removed my shirt to see what looked like claw marks on my side. I had bruises the shape of handprints, and it looked like I'd had some kind of surgery. At first this frightened me, but when I awoke the next day, the marks were gone. I felt as though God had performed His surgery on me and had removed the demonic influence that had locked onto me.

When I left Birmingham for home that weekend, I didn't realize that my battle wasn't over, that it was just beginning. God was working deliverance in me, but it wasn't instantaneous. Since my release from prison, I had continued to give in to my desire for drugs above my desire for God's presence in my life. God was willing to give me the freedom I had sought at the crusade in Birmingham, but He was holding it in reserve until I learned to put nothing else above Him.

Jesus tells us in the gospel of Matthew:

"Ask and it will be given to you; seek and you will

*find; knock and the door will be opened to you. For
everyone who asks receives; he who seeks finds; and
to him who knocks, the door will be opened."*

Matthew 7:7-8

This scripture passage shows us that there is a process in receiving answers to our prayers. God loves His children and will give us what we ask for if we are walking in obedience and in His will for our lives. When we ask while we are not living obediently in God's will, God holds our "yes" in reserve until we fulfill the next step of the process, which is to "seek." What is it that we're supposed to seek? We are to seek Him!

*"But seek first his kingdom and his righteousness, and
all these things will be given to you as well."*

Matthew 6:33

Have you ever had a friend in your life who only ever called you when he wanted a favor or wanted to borrow something? You don't mind helping that person out in the beginning, but when he continues to come to you for the same thing over and over, you begin to wonder if there's any real relationship between you or if he is only interested in what you can do for him. It's no different in our relationship with our Heavenly Father. He wants to know that we are sincere in our desire to love and serve Him. He asks us to seek a deeper relationship with Him (seek first His kingdom) and to prove it by walking in obedience (and His righteousness).

God knew that for my freedom to really stick in my life permanently, I would need to seek Him like never before, and He would allow the enemy to test me soon after my return home.

CHAPTER EIGHT

DIGGING UP YOUR "SEEK"

Hide your face from my sins and blot out all my iniquity. Create in me a pure heart, O God, and renew a steadfast spirit within me. Do not cast me from your presence or take your Holy Spirit from me.

Psalm 51:9-11

King David was a true worshiper of God. There was no casual, complacent faith in him—he was filled with a passion for God like no one before him. And God honored that passion by making David king of Israel over Saul and by establishing David's throne forever by making David's bloodline the one through which the promised Messiah would be born.

However, when King David wrote Psalm 51, he was going through a period of grief and remorse. He had sinned against God by committing adultery with Bathsheba and then having her husband killed in order to cover it up. When God sent the prophet Nathan to confront David about the seriousness of his sin, David became grieved by what he had done. He realized that he had allowed his own desires for fleshly things to come before his desire for that passionate relationship with God.

King David sincerely sought God's forgiveness and repented. At the time of his sin with Bathsheba, he had lost his desire to passionately seek God, but later, after having cleaned the slate with God, he began the process of digging up his "seek" once more.

Sometimes we Christians become so caught up in our needs and our desires that we lose sight of the real purpose of the Christian life, which is to seek the Lord and to seek Him passionately. Sometimes we forget that we are supposed to seek God simply for who He is rather than for what He can give us. If that happens, the Lord will take measures to remind us that He desires intimacy with us as both our Father and our Friend. The Lord tells us in the book of Jeremiah:

> *"You will seek me and find me when you seek me with all your heart. I will be found by you," declares the* Lord, *"and will bring you back from captivity."*
> Jeremiah 29:13-14

That's why the first commandment He gave us is to love the Lord our God with all our heart, soul, mind and strength. This is the essence of "seeking" Him. It's more than just being right with God—it's pursuing a relationship with Him passionately. Within that type of relationship, He is more than willing to give us what we need and want. When we seek Him with all we are and all we have, then the Lord is ready to deliver us from our own personal "captivity."

In Birmingham, my faith had been strong. I had been convinced God was going to instantly deliver me from my addictions and I had gone there seeking my freedom, but God had wanted more from me. He was willing to give me my freedom, but He was holding it in reserve for the day when I would desire Him and His ways more than the drugs and alcohol. When I got back home from Birmingham, God would allow me to be tested to see where my "seek" was really focused.

It seemed like the devil himself was waiting for me back in Georgia. A voice kept coming into my head telling me to test myself to see if I really was free from drugs. *How do you know*, it would say, *unless you try some to see if you still want it? Go buy some crack and try it to see if you really are free of it. If you're not free, you might need some more prayer.* Foolishly, I listened to the "reason" in that voice. I wanted to be sure there would never be the desire for drugs again, so I went looking for some. I realized later that the desire was still there or I never would have been willing to listen to that voice.

I went to the area of town where I could find the crack dealer, and even though I really didn't want any, I asked him to sell me some. The moment that I used it I instantly felt the wrath of Heaven shake above my car. I knew I had messed up because I felt God's presence leave me. There was nothing but cold emptiness inside me. I had no one to blame—I had chosen to walk in disobedience.

The next four weeks seemed like an eternity. I thought God had left me once and for all to die. I suddenly knew what King David had been feeling when he wrote in Psalm 51: *Do not cast me from your presence or take your Holy Spirit from me.* I was feeling incredible grief over having fallen into drugs again. I began to dig into my Bible seriously. I prayed to God, but felt nothing. I didn't realize that God will remove His presence from you to test you and to see where your heart really is concerning Him. (See Second Chronicles 32:31 and Isaiah 45:15). I continued to pray for other people too, but at the same time I was still doing the crack.

I knew I needed God's forgiveness and His deliverance. I also knew I would need help to find them, but getting help meant having to confess to someone that I had messed up again. I was having a hard time doing that.

Because I had signed the medical release at the crusade, Benny Hinn's follow-up team began to call me to check on my progress. Pastor Benny has an anointed, caring staff who follow up after his crusades with converts and with others who have been healed or delivered. They wanted to see me make it, but they also knew that the enemy is sneaky and would try to trip me up. When they began calling, I had already fallen and I could not bring myself to confess my failure to them. I had caller ID and refused to pick up when I knew it was them. I was running from every Christian everywhere in the belief that God was angry with me and wanted nothing more to do with me. I felt like Heaven had totally written me off. I cried out to God for over four weeks, but could get no answer from Him.

Thank God for my grandmother who had never failed to pray for me. She asked me one day if I was doing okay. I told her I was doing fine, but my grandmother has a gift of discernment. She knew I wasn't doing well, and she had a plan to help me. She asked me if I would take her, my grandfather, her sister and my father to the Benny Hinn crusade in November, which was being held in Orlando, Florida. I didn't want to go. I wanted God's presence in my life again, but every time I began to draw close to Him I would start to feel convicted about how I was living. But I finally agreed to take them. Somehow I knew that if I didn't get my life right, I was going to die.

We traveled to Orlando on November the fifth by car; I drove the whole way. I had been up the night before smoking crack all night long and could still smell and taste the drug in my system. That trip seemed like the longest 260 miles I'd ever traveled. My grandma, grandpa and great-aunt were all in their seventies, so we had to stop every thirty miles or so to go to the restroom or to stop at fruit stands and souvenir shops.

The crusade took place over that night and the next day. We had seats seven rows back from the front. We took our seats and as the worship began, I began to seek God—really seek Him—because I needed Him in my life again, because I missed His presence, because I knew that I was finally willing and ready to lay down everything just to be at His feet. The Holy Spirit began to wash over me, softening my heart and preparing my spirit for what would happen on the second day of the crusade.

On November sixth, the second day of the crusade, as worship time began again, a tremendous heaviness came over my heart. My sins began to play through my mind again. I saw how I had just played on the fringes of the flock, always returning to the things I wanted more than God. My heart broke. I began to cry right there with my family members beside me, but I didn't care. It was just me and the Lord in those moments, and

His presence was all around me. I repented right where I was, completely and sincerely, and holding nothing back.

Worship had ended and Pastor Benny was preaching and praying for people, but God was still dealing with me in my seat. As I was weeping and repenting, the power of God began to vibrate my body. Both of my hands went numb from the fingertips to the elbows. At first I thought something was physically wrong with me, but then I realized that God was working something in me. I was standing in His glory.

The human will can't survive the fire of God's glory. God is a consuming fire, and when you stand in His glory, He will burn that self-will right out of you. That's what was happening to me.

The service was nearing its end when Pastor Benny called for everyone who felt a call to the ministry to run down front for prayer. I couldn't ignore the urging of the Holy Spirit inside of me. I had to wiggle and push my way through a hungry crowd to get near the platform on the floor. As he was crossing the stage, Pastor Benny suddenly stopped and whirled around. His eyes began searching the crowd and quickly settled on me.

He said, "Young man! You in the brown shirt! Come up here!"

For a moment I was in shock and thought he couldn't really be talking to me. I glanced at the people around me with a look on my face that must have said, W*ho, me?*

"Get him up here." Pastor Benny instructed some of his ministry workers to bring me to the platform. They walked me up in front of him.

"Don't move," he told me, and then he turned away. My hands were really numb as all of this was going on, and I was trying to figure out how to get the feeling back in them while watching him at the same time. There were about 11,000 people watching, including the whole world, because parts of the crusade were being televised.

Suddenly Pastor Benny spun around and marched toward me with two fingers stuck out, and in that moment he said the words, "Father, anoint him!" Immediately I felt the fire of God flow into me like a hot, burning liquid. It flowed down my throat and into my stomach, and on settling there, it exploded inside of me like a stick of dynamite. I had never felt anything like it before, nor would I ever know anything like it since then. Instantly, I was delivered from my addictions. All my sensory memories of the drugs, alcohol and tobacco were gone.

I left the service that day and could not tell you what a glass of beer tasted like. It was as though I never had one. I couldn't remember the taste of a cigarette or any of the feelings associated with my drug use. God's anointing had broken the yoke that these things had bound me with. The Lord had released my deliverance because I had finally dug up my "seek" and had come to Him in repentance and brokenness, seeking Him and only Him.

My life would change from that point onward. Not only did He remove my memories of what the highs felt like and how the drugs smelled and tasted, but I couldn't even stand to be around the crowd I had hung with. I couldn't turn on the television set and watch the shows

I had always watched. God had burned the desire for those things right out of me and placed inside of me a desire for Him and for His ways. Suddenly I couldn't get enough Bible study. I couldn't get enough prayer. I couldn't get enough worship time. Not only did the Lord set me free from my bondages; He also filled me with a hunger for Him like I had never known before.

CHAPTER NINE

MAKING GOOD OUT OF BAD

And we know that in all things God works for the good of those who love him, who have been called according to his purpose. Romans 8:28

Basketball is a popular sport in this country. It's played on playgrounds, in schools, in colleges and on a professional level. One of the things learned in playing this game is that your team is supposed to score more points than the other team. However, the opposing team will attempt to keep you from scoring. Sometimes in the midst of trying to take away the ball, a member of the other team may "foul" you. Most fouls involve an illegal use of the hands or an illegal maneuver.

When you are fouled, you receive the right to step up to the free throw line and take two unopposed shots at the basket. The mistake made by your opponent has given you opportunity to advance your team's score.

This scenario happens often in the Christian life as well. Sometimes, when we are opposed by the enemy, he "fouls" us—bad things happen in our lives. But Christians who are in obedience training learn that they are able to take advantage of those fouls by turning them into opportunities to "score" for God's team.

Sometimes those "fouls," or bad things, that happened in our past can be used to help others find the Lord in the present or future. God is able to take the junk in our lives and turn it into an advantage that advances His Kingdom. He may even have allowed some of those circumstances in your life in order to train you for a particular destiny. If you're struggling with the "fouls" of the enemy today, consider the possibility that you are in training to help others through similar situations.

The apostle Paul explains it like this in the book of Romans:

> *Praise be to the God and Father of our Lord Jesus Christ, the Father of compassion and the God of all comfort, who comforts us in all our troubles, so that we can comfort those in any trouble with the comfort we ourselves have received from God. For just as the sufferings of Christ flow over into our lives, so also through Christ our comfort overflows.*
>
> 2 Corinthians 1:3-5

Because God strengthens and comforts us in the midst of our trials, He expects us to do the same for others who are caught in the same or similar circumstances. The comfort we receive from Him should overflow through Christ in us and out onto others. Our God is a compassionate God, and He wants His followers to be compassionate also.

If you've suffered from abuse in the past, but now you've found Jesus as your Savior, consider that your mission may be to minister to others who have been abused. If you've gone through a serious illness, think about the possibility that you may be called to minister to the sick. If you've been caught up in addictions to alcohol, drugs, pornography or something else, your ministry in Christ may very well be one of deliverance or of comfort to others who are addicted.

In the time following the Benny Hinn crusade in Orlando, I found another job and would spend my lunch hours in the Christian bookstore or reading my Bible. I was so hungry for God that I would spend my evenings going to church and revival services all across Georgia. If there was a service, I was there. I was on fire.

It wasn't long before the Lord gave me an opportunity to take the bad stuff that I'd gone through and turn it into good for His glory. The Lord began to work out the details of placing me into a local jail and prison ministry.

My own failures and difficulties had certainly been intended to keep me from finding salvation, and then later, to keep me from coming into my destiny as a minister of the Gospel. However, when I had been in prison, God had used me to minister to other prisoners. And, because God used my history of addictions and my incarceration when I was still in prison, I had no doubt that He could use them even more fully and powerfully now that I had been freed from prison and delivered from my addictions.

Through a divine appointment, I met a man who would become instrumental in my becoming involved in prison ministry. He came into the place where I worked one day looking for one of our products. He was involved in ministering to prisoners and found out that

I was newly released from prison myself. We developed a casual friendship, and in the course of time, he felt led of the Lord to give my name and address to inmates who were locked up with life sentences. He also purchased boxes of witness tracts, which explain the plan of salvation, and had them delivered to my house. I didn't understand all of this, but I knew God was about to do something in my life, so I simply said yes and stored the tracts, waiting to see what doors the Lord would open next.

The inmates who received my name and address began to write to me, asking me to minister to them through writing letters. These guys were desperate for a touch from anyone who cared. I began to feel compassion for them, desiring to give them hope in the midst of their hopelessness. Soon, I was spending my evenings writing pages and pages of letters, which took almost all of my free time in the evenings.

God continued to make connections for me. My letter ministry grew into a visitation ministry. I began to go to the jail twice a week after work. My pastor hooked me up with a jailer who opened doors for me to go into the prison in Tifton, Georgia, to minister, and because I had been in the same circumstances that many of these prisoners were experiencing, my words rang with authority for them. I had suffered as they were suffering, but I had found deliverance in a God who could do the miraculous, and the example of my life gave them hope. They believed that if I could find freedom and joy in Jesus, so could they.

Many prisoners came to know Christ through my testimony, but even more, as I prayed for them, were miraculously delivered from their bondages and addictions just as God had delivered me. Even some of the officers got saved. Sometimes the parents of these prisoners would call me on the phone afterward to ask me what I had done to their son or daughter. "They're different now," the parents would say, and I would begin to tell them about the power and presence of Jesus. Some of these parents received the Lord right over the phone.

None of this would have been possible without my obedience to the Lord. By then I had learned the basics of obedience: obey His Word, obey His voice, submit to His discipline and submit to His direction.

The first step in learning obedience requires that we know God's Word. If you don't know what God says about right and wrong, you can't live it, so it's essential that you study the Bible. Find out what God has to say about things like forgiveness, sexual immorality, drunkenness, slander and many other things. Although the Bible gives very clear direction on some issues, it may not give us specific answers for *every* issue we face, but in those cases it *does* give us guiding principles to follow.

The second step in learning obedience requires that we obey God's voice. This means learning how to hear and be led by the Holy Spirit. When Jesus walked this earth in His human body, He told His disciples that He only did what the Father told Him to do.

But the world must learn that I love the Father and that I do exactly what my Father has commanded me.
John 14:31

Because we are to live our lives as Christ lived His, we must also learn to do what the Father tells us to do.

God the Father communicates with us through the Holy Spirit, who lives inside of us. Learning to hear the Holy Spirit requires time spent in prayer.

Prayer consists of both talking to God and listening for God. Often those subtle thoughts that come to us while we are quiet in prayer are the leading of the Holy Spirit. So prayer is essential for learning how to hear the Holy Spirit.

How can we determine if an instruction is really from the Holy Spirit? One way is by knowing God's Word. God will never contradict Himself. If an instruction doesn't line up with the written Word, you can be assured that it isn't from God. Another way is through confirmations of that word from other sources. If you're unsure if an instruction is from the Lord, ask Him to send you confirmation of it. He will. Another way is through the consistency of that instruction. The Holy Spirit will continue to impress His instruction on your heart until you either accept or reject it. By following all three of these means of knowing the Holy Spirit's voice, you will become familiar with His voice.

Once you've learned how to hear God's voice, you should begin to step out in faith to do whatever He tells you to do. Has God told you to lay hands on someone who is sick and pray for their healing? Has God told you to give more than your tithe to your church? Has God told you to witness to your next-door neighbor? When we are faithful to perform what God instructs us to do, He will begin to entrust more to us every day.

The third step is to submit to God's discipline. *Discipline* can be another word for *training* or *teaching*. Submitting to God's discipline means giving up our own desires, our own wills, for His. We have to willingly lay aside what we want and take up what He wants. This also means walking out all the instructions and teachings learned in steps one and two. It's not enough just *knowing* what the Bible says about issues or just *hearing* what the Holy Spirit tells us to do, but we also then have to live out those teachings, principles and instructions every day.

Discipline also means correction. When we don't submit to God's teachings, He will then correct us. He may send others to challenge our disobedience, or He may send circumstances that will direct our lives back to Him. He may even allow us to walk in disobedience until we step into the snares of the enemy, which will cause us to remember how much better we had it when we were obedient.

The fourth step is to submit to God's direction. His direction is your destiny. God has a divine destiny planned for every life that He creates. Only after we receive Jesus as our Savior *and* Lord are we able to fulfill this destiny. I knew at a young age that I was called to minister the Gospel around the world, but this destiny couldn't be fulfilled until I gave myself entirely over to Jesus. We all make a choice to live life on our own terms or on God's terms. When we're able to surrender our own desires and allow God to have His way in us, He will begin to move us into the destiny He has planned for us.

When we learn these important steps and begin to walk in obedience, God will begin to entrust us with the work that He wants to do in the world.

God's work through me didn't stop at just the developing prison ministry. He had brought me out of brokenness into a place where I was hungry for Him. I told the Lord, "I will do anything You want me to do. I'll go anywhere You want me to go. I'll talk to anybody You want me to talk to. I will pray for people, Lord. Send me people who are sick. Send me opportunities for Your love and power to flow out of my body to be a testimony of Your love and grace."

I had left behind my life of occasional, convenient obedience and begun to walk in simple obedience—doing whatever God asked of me without question. Because of this, the Lord began to do the miraculous through my life.

Chapter Ten

Controlling Your Zeal

*Then Simon Peter, who had a sword, drew it and
struck the high priest's servant, cutting off his right
ear. (The servant's name was Malchus.)*

John 18:10

Peter is probably Jesus' best known disciple. One reason this is so is because of his passion and zeal for the Lord. It was Peter who didn't hesitate to jump out of the boat onto the stormy night waters of the Sea of Galilee and walk across the water, only to falter midway and be rescued by the Lord. It was also passionate Peter who was zealous enough to defend his Lord in the Garden of Gethsemane the night Jesus was arrested. As the scripture verse from the gospel of John tells us, Peter was the one who drew a sword, intending to defend the Lord through violence if necessary and cutting off the ear of the high priest's servant in the process.

What Peter missed that night, and what so many other new disciples often miss, is that we sometimes do things that are entirely contrary to what Jesus teaches simply because we allow our zeal for our newfound faith to overcome us. This is a trap new disciples of Christ need to beware of because those not-so-Christ-like actions or words we display in the midst of our zeal for the Lord can actually do the opposite of what we intend for them to do.

I nearly had one such incident in my life early on after my deliverance at the Benny Hinn crusade in Orlando. The whole event took place about the same time that the prison ministry was developing.

Things were going really great for me. The prison ministry was starting to take shape. I was praying for people and they were getting healed. In my zeal, I was preaching to anyone and everyone who would listen.

Just as they had after I had attended the first crusade in Birmingham, Benny Hinn's ministry staff followed up with me after the Orlando crusade. They began a process to document the miracle of deliverance from drugs and alcohol that I had experienced, in order to validate it as authentic. I was excited to help because I *wanted* people to know what God had done for me.

I was asked to take a drug test and fax the results to their doctor. I think I was probably the only probationer who begged his probation officer to give him a drug test! That's how zealous I was about the miracle God had performed in my life. My probation officer gave me the test. He signed it and we faxed it to Benny Hinn's ministry as they had requested. I also wrote out my testimony and sent that too.

A lady named Brenda with the ministry in Orlando encouraged me by telling me that they had faxed my testimony directly to Pastor Benny. Brenda's supervisor had suggested that I might be invited to testify at an upcoming crusade, and she passed that information along to me.

The next week that very thing happened. I received

a letter from the ministry telling me to let them know if I would be coming to any crusades in the future so they could inform Pastor Benny and the producer of his TV show. I got very excited about it, and I already had a level of new-Christian zeal that was above normal. I was so radical that I made Christian people nervous to be around me.

No one had taught me the Christ-like, ethical way to handle my excitement, so I was headed full speed into mistakes and misunderstandings that would take much work to clear up. I started calling Benny Hinn's ministry often to tell the follow-up team that I was coming to a crusade and would let them know when. Out of my excitement, I even called just to talk about Jesus. In reality, my behavior was raising red flags at the Orlando ministry. After all, they had documentation on my history: I was a thirty-eight-year probationer with a history of drug and alcohol abuse and had spent time in mental hospitals. I had charges of stalking, burglary, criminal trespass, forgery, possession of cocaine with intent to distribute, and many DUI's on my record. I perfectly fit the personality profile of a flake.

Fortunately, my life reflected something very different. God was really moving through me in dynamic ways to minister to and help people. But the miracles that God performed gave me more reasons to call them and share what was happening in my life. Then, to top it off, the ministry had taken a picture of me at the very crusade where I had been delivered and had randomly selected it for the back cover of Benny Hinn's quarterly magazine, *This Is Your Day*, so my excitement level went up again. I believed all this to be divinely orchestrated so that I could testify at a crusade.

Some friends of mine were going to go to a book signing where Benny Hinn was going to sign and give away copies of his newest book. I was not able to go, but I bought a copy and asked my friends if they would have him sign it for me. Not only did they get the book signed, but they also had the opportunity to share my testimony with Pastor Benny. He asked them for my contact information so he could invite me to testify at the next crusade. They called me at work to tell what had happened. The excitement and zeal rose another notch.

My friends phoned the Orlando ministry the next day and gave the contact information to a pastor's assistant. That assistant followed protocol and passed the information up the chain of command to Brenda's supervisor, who quickly brought it to a halt when she saw the records the ministry had on me.

Not long after, I received a phone call at work saying that I was not to come to a crusade for a while so they could check me out. The lady on the phone came across somewhat firm with me, telling me there was no way I was going to get on the platform to testify at this time, so I might as well stay home. After all the building up of excitement, this wasn't what I was expecting, so this news and her firmness knocked me out of the spiritual and into the flesh. I took offense at what she had told me, although I said nothing to her at that moment. But afterward, the old David Piper rose up in me and I suddenly felt like throwing in the towel and going back to my old way of living. I thought that if this was the way Christians treated one another, then it was no different than the life I had led before. (I never considered that perhaps her zeal to protect Pastor Benny from what she perceived as a threat was as great as my own zeal for the Lord.) I was overcome with thoughts of going home and doing drugs, and I started home from work with those exact intentions.

When I got home, I started to get ready to go out to "party" with my old drug-addicted friends when all of a sudden I noticed that the answering machine was flashing. There was a message on the line. To my surprise, the message was from a young lady I used to smoke crack with. She was crying and wanted me to call her back. I phoned her right away. The young lady told me that she'd heard I didn't do drugs any more, that I had a brand-new life, and she asked me to pray for her because she wanted Jesus to do the same for her.

I began to pray for her over the phone. As we prayed together, the presence and power of God began to fill my room and the old desire to do drugs left me instantly. I realized what I had been about to do and was thankful that the Lord had intervened by sending this phone call. God had provided a way of escape, just as He promises in His Word that He will do.

> No temptation has seized you except what is common to man. And God is faithful; he will not let you be tempted beyond what you can bear. But when you are tempted, he will also provide a way out so that you can stand up under it.   1 Corinthians 10:13

After the call ended, I found myself becoming indignant once more with the woman at the Orlando ministry for doubting that my testimony was valid. I felt as though she was casting doubt on a miracle of the Lord, and my zeal to defend that rose up again. So, I did a very foolish thing; I called that lady and left a foolish and not so nice message on her voice mail. I told her I was going to a crusade and there was nothing she or anybody else could do to stop me. (This was not the smart thing to do!)

The ministry team informed Pastor Benny of what had transpired, convincing him with my records that I was not mentally stable. He gave the order to have me removed from the crusade if I should show up. In the meantime, he asked one of his staff members and close associates, Pastor Dave, to check me out.

Pastor Dave called me one Friday night to talk, but I was still upset about the whole situation and didn't even give him a chance to say much of anything. No doubt he hung up the phone thinking the staff was right after all.

The date for the next crusade came up. It was scheduled to be in Memphis, Tennessee, and I planned to go. I knew they weren't going to let me testify, but I still wanted to be there among the worshipers, experiencing Pastor Benny's anointing. Before I left town to drive the 800 miles to get there, I went by my pastor's office to get a letter of reference from him stating that I was accountable, that I really was set free from drugs and that I was filled with an unusual zeal. When I got to Memphis, I went to the prayer meeting the ministry was holding the night before the actual crusade was to start. At the prayer meeting, ministry team members asked me if I would be an usher at the crusade. I was elated, thinking that perhaps my angry phone message had been forgotten and that I was forgiven.

Ushers were to report to the arena early, so I went the arena the next day in the afternoon. It was still several hours before the crusade was supposed to begin. As soon as I entered the arena through an entrance reserved for ushers, I heard my name called. A member of the ministry asked me to wait there because some-one needed to speak with me. Immediately I sensed that all was not forgotten as I had hoped. I waited for almost an hour, hearing the Lord tell me as I waited that I was about to be kicked out.

Then the crusade coordinator came to me, saying that he was sorry to be the bearer of bad news. He said they were unable to use me as an usher, and that, in fact, they were asking me not to come to the crusade at all. If I had any questions, I was to call the head of ministry security in about two weeks. He handed me a piece of paper with the phone number.

I was crushed. I had come 800 miles just to worship God, but because I had not known how to control my zeal for the Lord, I had acted immaturely by trying to go around the ministry's protocol. The result was that I got kicked out.

I was devastated but knew that I was the cause of it. I went downtown to sit in a café, and there I cried real tears and called out to God. As I sat there feeling sorry for myself, I remembered my pastor's letter of reference. I used the pay phone and called Pastor Dave's hotel room. His wife answered, and I didn't mean to, but I told her my whole story and she got upset. My call was coming right before the crusade was to start, and she was the organist. Pastor Dave got on the phone, un-happy that someone was upsetting his wife right be-fore she had to play. In spite of that, I managed to talk with him, and I told him about the letter of reference from my pastor.

"I need that letter," he told me. He gave me instruc-tions to drop the letter off at the front desk of his hotel and told me not to come to the crusade until the next day so he had time to get the whole mess straightened out. From our conversation, it was obvious to him that there had been some misunderstandings and a lack of communication, so his promise to try to help me was sincere.

I did as he asked and dropped the letter off at the hotel's front desk. I was on my way back to my hotel when I heard the Lord say, "I want you to go to the crusade." Now that I had lifted up my tears of repentance and had given my apologies to Pastor Dave, I was back on the track of living obediently again. God was giving me clearance to go to the crusade *today*, instead of waiting until tomorrow. Some of my friends had suggested that I just sneak into the crusade in disguise and lay low so I could enjoy the worship. Now God was telling me, "*Go.*"

I sneaked into the arena past the ministry team and went to the top, almost to the "nosebleed" section. I figured I would be safe up there as long as I stayed low and didn't draw any attention to myself. The service had already started and I found the last empty seat in the whole place—between a heavyset lady and an overly excited, nervous-looking man.

The service went on for over an hour with me wedged between this heavyset lady and "Mr. Can't Be Still." No one knew I was there but me and the Lord. Things were going fine until suddenly the unthinkable happened. Pastor Benny was telling us about a dream he'd had about Elijah, Oral Roberts and the blood of Jesus. The arena was so quiet that you could have heard a pin drop when all of sudden "Mr. Can't Be Still" jumped up out of his seat and began to scream at the top of his lungs that he was Elijah. "The spirit of Elijah has come and I am he!" he shouted.

I tried in vain to shut him up. "What are you doing,

you crazy man! Sit down!" But he just screamed all the more. Every TV camera and light in the place focused on us, and every eye in the arena turned to see who was yelling that he was Elijah. And who did they see sitting there but "Mr. Elijah" *and me*—"Mr. Elisha", who wasn't allowed in the crusade. "Mr. Elijah" then took off running like a madman.

I stayed in my seat like a good boy, kept my voice low, kept my eyes down and prayed. I thought for sure my cover was about to be blown. But the Lord had given me His blessing to come to the crusade and He protected my cover. The ministry team members were so focused on catching the crazy man that they never paid any attention to me. I thanked God for the blessing of being allowed to stay for the rest of the service.

The next day, my problems with the Benny Hinn ministry were straightened out. Pastor Dave had read the letter from my pastor and showed it to the right people. We met and Pastor Dave hugged me, telling me how sorry they were about all the misunderstandings and that they loved me and were truly excited about all God had done in my life.

If I had controlled my zeal and had acted like Jesus, with meekness, humility and forgiveness, then all of this could have been avoided in the first place. But I had acted in the flesh and had refused to submit to the spiritual authority of others, which showed my own immaturity. I grew from this experience and learned a hard lesson about controlling my zeal and not taking offense.

CHAPTER ELEVEN

DISCOVERING YOUR DESTINY

In his heart a man plans his course, but the LORD determines his steps. Proverbs 16:9

God created every one of us with a built-in destiny, and the choices we make in life determine if we will discover and fulfill that destiny or if we will derail it. Those choices always revolve around our obedience or disobedience to what God has called us to do. As we learn to walk obediently before Him, God begins to open more doors of opportunity.

What Proverbs 16:9 (shown above) tells us is that God opens and closes your doors of opportunity. The best way to receive open doors of opportunity is to show God that you can be trusted with the responsibilities that lie on the other side of those open doors. When you walk in obedience to Him, you show Him that you are reliable and He will then begin to increase your opportunities. This principle is illustrated in Jesus' parable of the talents in Matthew 25.

In the parable, the property owner called his three servants together. He was going away on a trip and he put them in charge of increasing his finances while he was away. He gave a portion to each servant. He gave the first servant five talents, the second servant two talents, and the third servant one talent, and he gave these talents to each servant *"each according to his ability."* This tells us that the property owner already knew the abilities of each servant. How did the property owner know their abilities? He could only have known from previous experience in entrusting them with responsibility! From this scripture, we can conclude that the property owner would have given his most trusted servant the most talents, the second most reliable servant the second highest number of talents, and the least reliable servant the least number of talents.

When the owner returned from his trip, his most trusted servant had doubled the money given to him. The second servant had also doubled the money given to him. The third servant had failed to follow through and returned only what was given to him from the start. Because he had proven himself unreliable with it, the talent he had received was taken away from him. For their trustworthiness, the other two servants received their master's praise. This passage then tells us that the master promised to give both of the reliable servants charge over many other things because they had proven themselves faithful and obedient with what they had been given. In other words, he would give them more opportunities to be faithful with.

(You may wonder why the owner gave that one talent to the third servant at all when he knew that servant was unreliable. He did it because he was offering that servant a second chance to prove faithful. This point illustrates that our God is also a God of second chances. He will continue to give you opportunities to walk in obedience until the end of the age. After that there will be no more second chances, which is reflected in the end of the parable.)

When you walk in obedience to the Lord, you prove to Him that you are reliable with the things He has given you and with the things He has called you to do. When you prove reliable, the Lord is quick to reward you with open doors of opportunity that lead to greater responsibilities. He will order your steps in such a way that you will begin to walk in the purposes for which He created you. You will then be on the way to discovering your destiny.

When I began to move down the path of obedience, the Lord began to open new doors for me that would begin to lead me into my destiny. Not long after the crusade in Memphis and when the prison ministry was starting to take off, God gave me opportunities to prove faithful.

One day my phone rang. It was ringing every day by this time, but this call in particular was sent from the Lord as a "talent" that I was to be obedient with. A young lady who was faithfully going to church and serving the Lord told me that her daddy, who had been clean and sober for twelve years off of drugs, was now smoking crack again. He had begun to beat up his kids and he was out of control. She said, "Please pray for my daddy."

I said, "Let's pray a tough prayer." She agreed, so we prayed together. "Father, take everything he's got, even if it means locking him up. Do whatever it takes to bring him back to You, but Lord, please spare his life. Save him and fill him with the Holy Ghost and use him in the ministry. In Jesus' mighty name. Amen!"

Thirty days later, Richard Douglas, this young lady's

daddy, barricaded himself inside of his mobile home, loaded his 12-gauge shotgun, put it under his chin and pulled the trigger. When I heard what had happened, I went straight to the hospital. Richard was in intensive care, lying in the bed nearly lifeless. His head was swollen up to the size of a basketball. His tongue was swollen and sticking out of his mouth. He was on a breathing machine.

As I stood beside Richard's bed, I clearly heard the Lord say, "In fourteen days, I will raise him up." I knew the Lord was giving me this word in direct response to our prayer a month before. I also knew the Lord wasn't telling me this so I would keep it to myself. He was planning to do a miracle for this man, but in order for that miracle to bring Him glory, I would have to speak out His word to me.

I called up my friends Paul and Linda McGrath, whom I knew were used to hearing such messages from the Lord, and I asked them to pray for Richard. I didn't tell them what I had heard from God. During our prayer time together on the phone, they heard from the Lord and told me, "We hear two weeks. God will raise him up in two weeks." They were giving me confirmation. I knew what the Lord was asking me to do, so I went back to the hospital that same day.

When I got there, Richard's family was there, our pastor was there, and church friends were there. I walked into the room where all these people were gathered and I spoke what God had told me to say, "Thus says the Lord God of Israel, in fourteen days Richard Douglas will be raised up, healed, delivered, set free and saved." Our pastor tried to hush me up, but I knew what the Lord had told me and I knew He would do what He promised to do. I spoke directly to Richard's mother then. She was not a born again believer. "God is not going to take your son. In fourteen days, God is going to raise him up again." They ran me out of the hospital. I went to work and didn't worry about it again because I had no doubt whatsoever that the Lord would perform what He had spoken.

The promise of the Lord is always true. In fourteen days, Richard awoke. He began to cry, and he accepted Jesus as his Savior. The doctors said that even so Richard wouldn't walk for maybe a year, but God had other plans for the man. Thirty days after he had pulled the trigger on the shotgun, Richard was not only walking, but he went water-skiing! He later went with me to the jail several times to minister with me and testify to the inmates of what a miracle-working God we serve. Today he has a music ministry, writing songs for Jesus, and has even put out his own CD!

I had asked God to move in Richard's life and in response, God had asked me to take part of the responsibility of that request by speaking out His word so He would get the glory for changing Richard's life. Because I had proven faithful in this, God would give me another opportunity very soon after that to prove faithful again.

One evening I came home from work and headed to the jail ministry. Afterward, I stopped by my grandma's house. She had a meal waiting for me even though it was late. As soon as she saw me, she told me, "Your cousin Larry had a stroke. They don't expect him to make it through the night." I had been an outcast of the family for so long before getting right with the Lord that I didn't even know who cousin Larry was. I had always been in jail or hanging out with my druggie friends when the rest of the family would get together for re-unions. She told me he was in the hospital in Albany and gave me his room number. Albany was about forty miles from where we were and I had been there earlier in the day. I heard the Lord distinctly say to me, "Go and I'll heal him."

It was eleven o'clock at night. Albany was an hour's drive away and I had to be at work by eight o'clock in the morning. I thought, *Lord, why didn't You tell me about this when I was there earlier?* But it's the incon-venient things that God asks you to do that are the most anointed. When you get out of your flesh and go in spite of the cost or inconvenience, then an anointing goes with you.

The Lord told me, "If you'll go tonight, I will heal this man and use this miracle to expand your ministry in your hometown. I went, and the closer my car got to that hospital, the stronger the anointing on me grew.

It was very late when I arrived. I had to sneak into the hospital, all the while praying the hospital security guards wouldn't see me and stop me. When I got to cousin Larry's room, the door was half open already, so I pushed it open and entered the room. Larry's wife, Betty, his son and his daughter were there, and though I didn't remember them very well, they certainly re-membered me and they weren't happy to see me. The David they remembered had been a crack addict, alco-holic and thief. Betty even hid her purse behind her, thinking maybe I was there to find money for drugs.

I told them I had come to pray for Larry. Betty told me my grandmother had already come to pray for him and that they had already prayed for him. They were Baptist.

I said, "No, Ma'am. God sent me over here. Sometimes He uses me in special ways." Just to humor me so I'd leave quicker, they agreed to pray.

Larry was strapped down on the bed. Due to the effects of the stroke, he was kicking and trying to pull the IVs out. He had been like that all day.

We joined hands and formed a circle around the bed and began to pray. The moment I said the name of Jesus, a light filled the room. There seemed to be an electric charge in the air. I knew something was happening, so I opened my eyes and saw a blue mist hovering over the bed. I wasn't the only one to see it. Betty also saw it. A short time later, Larry was still, and when I left he was sleeping like a baby.

They told me later that he had awakened at 5:00 AM and asked, "Where am I?" When the doctors ran some tests on him, they could find no evidence that he had ever had a stroke. He was discharged from the hospital the next day. At the time, Larry wasn't even saved, but I had not known that.

After that, Betty, who was known by many people in Albany and in my hometown area, told everyone she knew that the old David Piper was dead and that God had raised him up as a new man. She told them God had used me to heal her husband. But I wouldn't allow anyone to praise me. The glory belonged to the Lord and to Him alone, and I made sure I gave it all over to Him.

Today, Larry is serving God. In fact, he received Jesus as his Savior at one of my services. God allowed me to have a part in two miracles in Larry's life.

Because I had proven faithful in what He had asked, God began to put together opened doors of opportunity for a life in full-time ministry. The prophecy spoken over me at age twelve was slowly beginning to be fulfilled a reality because I had learned to be obedient to God. Several key people I would soon meet would play an important role in my journey toward the fulfillment of that prophecy.

CHAPTER TWELVE

ANSWERING THE CALL

Through him and for his name's sake, we received grace and apostleship to call people from among all the Gentiles to the obedience that comes from faith.

Romans 1:5

The life of obedience to God can be compared to the starting out of a train on a journey. The engine goes nowhere as it sits at the station. First the engine has to be started. Then the wheels begin to slowly turn and pull the train out of the station. The train seems to take a long time to gain speed, but once it finally gets up to speed it moves along at a constant, steady pace, chugging powerfully forward.

So it is with the life of obedience. We start out in reluctant obedience, loading our minds with God's Word only when it is convenient, obeying Him only when it suits our own agendas. If you're living at this level of obedience, you will always be stuck at the station, going nowhere in finding your divine purpose and fulfilling your destiny.

As we determine in our hearts to get started in living out *all* of God's principles for His followers, regardless of whether it is convenient and comfortable, then we are getting our engines started. Then we need to slowly learn how to study His Word and hear the voice of the Holy Spirit who teaches us and guides us. That's the slow process of turning our wheels and pulling out of the station. And then, we come to a place in our lives where we consistently live as Christ taught us we should and we follow through on the instructions given to us by God through His Spirit. This is the constant, steady chugging along of the train.

I call this level of the Christian walk "simple obedience." It's not "simple" because it's easy to get to this level. On the contrary, getting to this level can be very hard. I call it simple because the principle of it is so uncomplicated: if God says do it, then you do it; if God says don't do it, then you don't do it. This principle is much easier said than done, but once you reach this level of faith, that's when you are ready to step into the purposes for which God created you.

You may have discovered your destiny at this point or you may not have found it quite yet, but until you are living at a level of simple obedience, you won't be ready to answer the call that God has on your life. In order to *successfully* fulfill God's call on your life, you need to be living at the level of simple obedience. Once you are at this level, the Lord will set people along your path as road signs to guide you toward fulfilling your divine purpose. Even then, you have to be ready and willing to answer the call.

As the hunger for God grew in my life and as my ministry began to grow in my home area, the Lord put several people in my life to guide me into my divine destiny, but even then, I wasn't sure about answering that call.

It was mid-May 1999 when I heard about the revival meetings in Brunswick, Georgia, where the preacher was rumored to have gold sparkles appearing all over him miraculously while he ministered. I heard about him one day while I was getting my hair cut in the barber's chair. Immediately the Holy Spirit within me began to witness that this man was a God-fearing servant and that the miraculous sign of the gold was of God. Like some of the others I knew, I wanted to go see it for myself. So, I determined to go visit the Brunswick Revival to hear Bob Shattles speak.

I made it to one of the services around the first of June. I wanted to get there early enough to get a front row seat or one as close to the front as I could get. As it turned out, I was the first one there besides the ministry team workers. I asked a few of them who Bob Shattles was. They told me how he had been a police officer in Atlanta, but God had called him into the ministry and now he was preaching the Gospel. They told me that a lady prophet of God named Ruth Heflin had laid hands on this ex-policeman and God had begun to rain down this gold dust on him while he preached as a sign and wonder to unbelievers.

During the service that night, Bob Shattles walked up to me and said, "Young man, stand up." I stood, wondering what was about to come. Bob then said, "The Lord says you and I have been in some of the same places." That made sense to me because I had been a drug addict and he had been a policeman. "The Lord also says you are headed to the same place I am." This part of his prophetic word didn't click with me. Although it fit perfectly with other prophecies that had been spoken over me, I just wasn't quite ready to believe this was what God wanted for me.

During that service, I saw many people getting saved, healed and delivered. I knew that only the presence of God could do these things, so I knew Bob was for real, but I thought for sure that he couldn't have been right about me going to the same place he was, which was full-time ministry.

I thought Bob Shattles couldn't have possibly gotten his prophecy to me right. After all, I was still on thirty-eight years' probation and working a full-time job selling cars. Judging from my current circumstances, I couldn't possibly be headed to the same place he was, even though I was enjoying doing the jail ministry.

Soon after that, my life began to rearrange itself without any help from me. People began to come to me at the car lot looking for prayer instead of cars. My boss decided to give me an ultimatum: serve him or serve God. I chose God. I left his office mad that day, but glad at the same time. I felt as though this had been a good thing and that God was at work doing something in my life. I soon found another job and continued serving the Lord first.

I was right about God doing something in my life. News had begun to get around about how God was using me to heal and deliver people. Several pastors in the area had begun to hear about the healings and miracles that happened when I prayed for people, and my phone started ringing. They began to ask me to pray for people in hospitals, nursing homes, private homes and other places.

I continued traveling to Brunswick to hear Bob Shattles preach, as well as to Orlando to hear Pastor Benny Hinn. In Pastor Benny's Orlando church, I had met and become friends with a married couple named Paul and Linda McGrath. They would invite me to stay with them when I was in Orlando for Pastor Benny's services. They became a great asset in my life by speaking words of wisdom to me. Paul and Linda became my prayer warriors because they sensed the calling on my life.

Also at the Orlando church, I had met another couple, Rick and Bette Strombeck, who were (and still are) missionaries to Kiev. Bette sometimes helped Pastor Benny out during crusades to other countries due to her ability to speak several other languages fluently. At that time they were serving in Pastor Benny's church. I had struck up a conversation with them one day in the church parking lot and found out that Rick liked to hunt in the area where I lived. We had become great friends.

One day while driving down I-95 in Florida, the Holy Spirit directed me to drive to the beach. I did just as I was directed to do. I went up and down every road He led me down, even getting my car stuck in the sand at the beach at one point and having a couple of parties helping push me out. Just as the sun was beginning to go down and I was wondering why in the world God had told me to come this way, I saw a sign along the road with the name of a church on it. It caught my eye because that church had the exact same name as my home church: New Covenant Church of God. At once the Holy Spirit told me to turn around and go back to that church.

I did a U-turn and drove into the parking lot of the church to see people going into the building. Many of them looked to be homeless, or looked like drug addicts. I got out of the car, went inside and asked to see the pastor. They directed me to a man who was just walking into the building. I was surprised to see that he was a Santa Claus look-alike. He had long white hair and a beard just like Santa. I told him that I was an ex-drug addict and that God was using me in ministry to others. I explained that the Lord had directed me here for some reason but I wasn't sure why.

He told me that the people I saw were here for a feeding program he had been running. The requirement was that they had to sit through a church service before they could eat. He asked me if I would like to preach to them that day. The service was just about to start. If I had been any sooner or later, I would have missed this opportunity to minister to these people, but God had known the right timing and had guided me up and down streets to put me here at exactly this moment.

I told the pastor a little of my testimony, including how I had been delivered by God's power through Pastor Benny's ministry. This pastor didn't believe that God was really using Benny Hinn and didn't believe that most of what he saw on Pastor Benny's television program was real. But he was willing to let me speak because of my testimony.

The pastor was to speak first, so I went in and sat down. The room was full of homeless people, prostitutes and drug addicts. It was obvious that they were there for natural food, not because they were hungry for Jesus.

The pastor's sermon was forceful, loud and filled with condemnation—all hellfire and brimstone. There was no presence of the Holy Spirit in the room the entire time he preached.

After he had finished, he introduced me. I walked up to the front and looked out over about one hundred people and saw myself about eight months earlier. My heart was filled with compassion for these people. I knew why they had come, but they didn't know why I had come. They were about to find out.

I lifted my eyes toward Heaven and simply said, "Holy Spirit, You are welcome here." Their eyes all fixed on me because my words were not in the tone they had expected. I asked them, "How many of you know you can't see God right now?" All hands went up. Then I asked, "How many of you know you can feel God?" Only a few hands went up. Lastly, I asked, "How many of you *want* to feel Him right now?" All hands in the room went up. I told them to repeat after me. With all hands up and all eyes lifted like mine were, they all repeated after me, "Holy Spirit, we welcome You. Let us know You are real. Come, Holy Spirit."

All of a sudden the power of God hit the room like a strike of lightning. The room felt like it was filled with electricity, so much so that I thought the paint would melt right off the walls. I opened my eyes with tears streaming down them.

People in the room began to experience healing. I gave an altar call and everyone in that room gave their hearts to Jesus that day. Everyone at the altar had tears running down their cheeks, including that pastor and his altar workers. People were getting saved, delivered and healed. I left that church that day on top of the world.

One month later when I was again in Orlando, I sat and told Rick and Bette about this experience. We were looking at a map of the area and I pointed out to them about where the church was. Rick and Bette were very excited. They asked the name of the church. We found out that day that the pastor of the church where I had spoken was a large supporter of their ministry to the former Soviet Union. They had been praying for God to show this man that the work He was doing through

Benny Hinn was real. Incredibly, God had used me to do it. This convinced Rick and Bette beyond any doubt that God had great plans for my life. They became even greater supporters of me and looked for opportunities for me to minister.

Right after that trip to Orlando, God really began to speed up the pace of my "train." Two area pastors invited me to share my testimony in their churches. One of these pastors began to have me back every week. He called my night to preach "Thirsty Thursday." This lasted for a month. Then God told me this door would be closing but another would be opening. The last day of the "Thirsty Thursday" meetings my phone rang. A call came from a pastor in a town forty-five minutes away, asking me to come and minister at his church.

With all of these opportunities coming my way, I began to get more and more miserable at my secular job. God was speaking to my heart about going into full-time ministry, just as Bob Shattles had prophesied. Now I was finally able to accept and embrace that word. The Lord impressed on me that not only would I minister on a full-time basis, but that He would open up opportunities to me that would take me around the world.

I decided to take a week off work to think about what I should do. When I told my boss that I felt God calling me into full-time ministry, he pulled his pay stub out of a drawer and showed me his six-figure income. He asked if I was sure I wanted to be a preacher. I knew the answer. I said yes gladly, and I walked away from my job. That day I told the Lord that I was His fully and asked Him to use me however He saw fit.

I went home and told my dad that I had quit my job to go into full-time ministry. He immediately got scared for me. He thought I was making a mistake and that lack of a regular job and a regular income would lead me back into the drug life. He said, "No one knows you're a preacher. How can you preach?"

When I told my pastor, I faced more doubt about my decision. Even my friends in Orlando thought my decision was a little too quick and told me I needed to rethink it. After all, how could I preach around the world if no one knew me?

No preaching opportunities came, and I began to wonder myself if I had been too hasty. As my money began to run out, I took the last of it and went to Brunswick where Bob Shattles was still preaching the revival there. I was hoping for a miracle. I went to services there the entire week and still no doors opened for me. On Friday, the last day of the revival services for that week, I lifted my eyes to Heaven and prayed, "Father God, I know what You told me. If You don't open a door for me to minister soon, then everyone will say, 'I told you so.' They will believe they were right and I will have to go back to my old job."

That day, Paul and Linda McGrath had come to town from Orlando for the Brunswick services. They met me for lunch, where they told me that they had to go by a certain ministry in town called Messianic Vision to visit some friends. They asked if I wanted to go along.

When we got there, they asked me to wait in the foyer of that ministry's business office while they met with someone. I sat there for hours, wondering how and what I was going to do. I had very little money left. I had quit my job and had nowhere to preach. As I was waiting in my misery, a man walked in and sat down by me. He introduced himself as John Fuggiano. He was an evangelist to South America. We began to talk, and I shared my testimony with him. John said he felt the

Lord impressing upon him to tell me about a camp ministry in Virginia where people could stay for free. They would even feed you at no cost. He felt I should go there and wrote down on paper the name and phone number of someone there I should contact. I put the paper in my pocket. That night after services, I gathered up my Bible and was headed out to my car when a man and his wife walked up to me asking, "Young man, are you a preacher?" He said he was the pastor of a church in a nearby small town and his wife had insisted that I was a preacher and was supposed to minister at their church. I was amazed at God's timing. That night I went home with a place to preach. God had opened my first door. I had answered the call and I was now in full-time ministry. Soon I would be launched into fulfilling that prophecy spoken over me as a child, and it would begin with that little piece of paper in my pocket.

CHAPTER THIRTEEN

RECEIVING THE PROMISES

If you fully obey the LORD your God and carefully follow all his commands I give you today, the LORD your God will set you high above all the nations on earth. All these blessings will come upon you and accompany you if you obey the LORD your God.

Deuteronomy 28:1-2

Just as those who disobey God are promised disciplinary measures (the Bible sometimes calls these curses), those who obey God are promised abundant blessings. The Lord gave the promise shown above to the nation of Israel through Moses. As a follower of Christ, you too are qualified to receive all the blessings of the Lord because you have been adopted into God's family.

I encourage you to open your Bible to read Deuteronomy 28 so you can see for yourself the list of the many blessings God promises to those who are obedient to Him. You can call these perks, or benefits.

One such benefit of living a life of obedience is that you will receive God's mercy. Merriam-Webster's online dictionary defines *mercy* as "a blessing that is an act of divine favor or compassion."

> *[I, the LORD, show] mercy to thousands, to those who love Me and keep My commandments.*
>
> Exodus 20:6 NKJV

> *And I said: "I pray, LORD God of heaven, O great and awesome God, You who keep Your covenant and mercy with those who love You and observe Your commandments, please let Your ear be attentive and Your eyes open."*　　　Nehemiah 1:5-6 NKJV

The greatest mercy He gives us is everlasting life. God promises that those who are obedient to His Word will never die. This refers to an eternity in Heaven in the presence of God instead of eternal damnation.

> *"I tell you the truth, if anyone keeps my word, he will never see death."*　　　John 8:51

A second benefit to obeying the Lord is that God promises to grant you the answers to your prayers.

> *Dear friends, if our hearts do not condemn us, we have confidence before God and receive from him anything we ask, because we obey his commands and do what pleases him.*　　　1 John 3:21-22

A third benefit you can receive for your obedience is prosperity. Merriam-Webster describes *prosperity* as "the condition of being successful or thriving, especially economic well-being." Does this mean that God will make you rich? Not necessarily, but it does mean He will grow and progress your finances as well as other things He has given you stewardship over.

> *He does not take his eyes off the righteous; he enthrones them with kings and exalts them forever.*
> *If they obey and serve him, they will spend the rest of their days in prosperity and their years in contentment.*   Job 36:7, 11

This passage from Job also tells us the obedient will be given favor with *"kings,"* meaning those who are in authority.

A fourth benefit of obedience is the healing of illness and disease. As part of His covenant with the children of Israel, the Lord promised healing.

> *If you pay attention to these laws and are careful to follow them, then the LORD your God will keep his covenant of love with you, as he swore to your forefathers.*
> *The LORD will keep you free from every disease. He will not inflict on you the horrible diseases you knew in Egypt, but he will inflict them on all who hate you.*
>   Deuteronomy 7:12, 15

In fact, your obedience is such a powerful key to releasing blessings from Heaven that even your children and your *"children's children"* can be blessed by it.

> *But from everlasting to everlasting the LORD's love is with those who fear him, and his righteousness with their children's children—with those who keep his covenant and remember to obey his precepts.*
>   Psalm 103:17-18

The blessings listed here are just a few of the promises God makes to those who are obedient to Him. There are many other blessings given in God's Word.

The blessings in my life began to accelerate when I pulled that piece of paper out of my pocket and dialed the number of the camp the fellow at Sid Roth's ministry had given me. I found out that it was true that I could come to the camp and stay free of charge. They had Pentecostal campmeetings every Friday and Saturday night and on Sunday mornings and evenings. During the summers, they held campmeetings daily during the months of July and August. It was a summer-long revival and it sounded exactly like what I needed.

I began to pray that the Lord would give me favor with the courts so that I could get permission to go. Also, because I had no money, I asked God for enough funds to make the trip. It must have been the Lord's will for me to go because He answered my prayers soon afterward. I received permission to go to Virginia from the probation office. Other people who were supportive of me had also been praying for me to be able to go. My phone began ringing as word got out among them, and soon people began to send me money in obedience to the Lord. I received $800.00 in less than twenty-four hours. I packed my car and took off for Ashland, Virginia.

I didn't know before I arrived at the camp that I would end up having to sleep on the ground in a tent in ninety-degree weather, spraying myself with bug spray, taking showers at a nearby gym, and brushing my teeth out of the trunk of my car. But I didn't really care because I knew God had wanted me to come here for a reason and I was determined to see what He had in store for me.

The camp director's name was Ruth Ward Heflin. Ruth Heflin had traveled the world as a missionary, prophetess and worship leader. She had prophesied to kings, emperors and heads of state in many nations. She was well respected and many people were in awe of her, including me. God would begin to give me favor with "Sister Ruth," as everyone called her, and she would become someone very influential in my life.

I went to every service, and every time there was a prayer line I was in it. There were different guest ministers throughout the time I spent there, but it didn't matter to me who was preaching. I would go to the altar each time to receive whatever the Lord wanted me to have. I lay on the floor at the front of the tabernacle in that Heaven-like spiritual atmosphere (they called it "the glory") and I soaked it all up like a dry sponge.

One day I felt the Lord calling me to go speak with Sister Ruth. I went to talk with her personal assistant, Connie Wilson, to ask how I could meet with her. Connie told me that summer camp season was very busy and that the pace of the campmeetings necessitated that Sister Ruth rest when she could. She said it was not likely that I would get to speak with her. She suggested I go to the office around 11:00 AM and ask them to call her. I did just as she said. The office staff called her, but did so reluctantly. The response came that I could have only twenty minutes to talk with her.

I went to Sister Ruth's house with butterflies in my stomach. I knew God had spoken to me to speak with her, but I was nervous just the same. I was given entrance to her home and found myself facing Sister Ruth herself in her living room.

She invited me to come in and sit down, and then asked me very plainly what I needed from her. I was terrified inside. Here I was sitting in front of the lady who was the greatest visionary and most respected prophetess in the world.

She asked me again why I had wanted to see her. I told her I wanted to share my testimony. She told me to go ahead and share it with her because she was so busy during camp season and she only had twenty minutes to give me.

I began to share what God had done for me by delivering me from drugs and how He had begun to open doors for ministry to me in my community. As I spoke, the power of God came into the room with us. She began to be moved by the presence of the Holy Spirit as He slowly filled up the room and changed the atmosphere where we were sitting. God had begun to speak to her concerning His plans for me. All of a sudden my hands began to burn like they had been submerged into hot, hot water. I knew I was receiving some kind of special impartation from Heaven. When I finished my testimony, she asked me to pray for her, and at the end of our meeting, she gave me a kiss on the cheek and told me she loved me. As we were walking out, she offered me her personal phone number in case I needed prayer or guidance. God had begun to knit us together in a wonderful mentoring relationship. Little did I know what else God was about to do for me through Sister Ruth.

The last week of summer camp was there before I knew it. By this time, I had actually grown to like sleeping in a tent on the ground (except for the heat and the bugs!). I was wondering what would come next for me as I went to the next to last meeting of the camp.

At that meeting, Sister Ruth announced she would be giving out ordination papers and Christian worker papers to those who were ready for such credentials. This was the custom at the end of summer camp. I prayed to the Lord at that moment, telling Him that I would like to have a ministry license under Sister Ruth's great ministry.

I got up and went to one of the camp workers, another sister who was close to Sister Ruth, and told her of my desire to be licensed. I thought it was enough to simply make the request. She looked very surprised and explained that it wasn't that simple. Sister Ruth was always very careful about whom she licensed. It sometimes took many years for someone to earn the privilege of being licensed under the ministry there. She offered to put in a good word for me to help me get Christian worker's papers. I was disappointed, but I told her that I understood.

The last day of camp I went to the service in which the list of names of those who were to be licensed would be read. I was very surprised when my name was read. I went up to receive my license and to be prayed for by the ministry team. Sister Ruth then charged us to go forth and preach the Word of God.

That summer was life-changing for me. God had showered His blessings on me, not only to continue in full-time ministry, but to do so with a license from and the backing of a well-respected ministry.

And now that God had equipped me with credentials to go preach His Word, He would soon open the biggest door I had yet experienced, leading to greater opportunity and even greater blessings.

CHAPTER FOURTEEN

TELLING OTHERS ABOUT GOD'S GOODNESS

Then Jesus came to them and said, "All authority in heaven and on earth has been given to me. Therefore go and make disciples of all nations, baptizing them in the name of the Father and of the Son and of the Holy Spirit, and teaching them to obey everything I have commanded you. And surely I am with you always, to the very end of the age."

Matthew 28:18-20

Sharing your story with others can be an exhilarating experience. Once you've made the U-turn from disobedience to obedience and your life has been transformed, you have an obligation to share your story with others. If God has brought you out of a broken life into the blessings of His goodness, then He can and will do the same for everyone. You should be ready and willing at this point to show your love for others by sharing with them how God helped you into a life of blessing.

Jesus came to this earth to teach us that the path of

obedience is the only road to the place of blessing. That's why He left His disciples with the final instructions you see in the passage from Matthew at the beginning of this chapter.

It's God's greatest desire to be in relationship with us and to bless us, but God cannot bless disobedience. Remember how I used my own children as an example in the first chapter? When my children disobey me, do I reward them? Of course not! When they disobey me, they are out of right relationship with me. Their disobedience shows me disrespect, which seriously strains our relationship. But when they obey me, they show me that they desire to please me and we have a good relationship. In these circumstances, it is my delight to bless my children with gifts and treats, or to find other ways to show them how special they are to me. This is the essence of God's relationship with us as well.

Don't misunderstand any of what we're saying here. I'm not telling you that performing a certain ritual or behaving a certain way will earn you God's favor. Relationship isn't built on obedience; it's reflected in it. I know the difference between my kids doing things to butter me up in order to get presents and my kids doing things because they love and respect me. God knows the difference, too.

God desires that every man, woman and child come to know Him in an intimate relationship, but most people don't understand this or have never heard this message. The Bible says,

My people are destroyed from lack of knowledge.
Hosea 4:6

Jesus left His last instructions in order to remedy that

problem. We are to share our knowledge of how to know God. When you know that having a right relationship with God and receiving His blessings comes from living in obedience to His Word, you need to obediently tell others this marvelous news. Jesus did not make this His final *request;* He made it His final *commandment.* And we are to be obedient even in this.

I had already learned the thrill of sharing how God had transformed my life. I was sharing my testimony everywhere I went with anybody who would listen. My desire to share Jesus grew so big that it became my passion, my call, my all-consuming need. The day came when I not only believed the word spoken over my life when I was a boy, that I would preach in many nations like the apostle Paul, but I desired for it to become a reality in my life. I wanted to go to the nations with the wonderful message of how God transforms, heals and delivers those who will follow Him. God saw this desire in my heart and knew I was ready to be released to preach in other nations.

In December 1998, before I had gone to hear Bob Shattles in Brunswick and before I had met Ruth Heflin, when I was just getting the jail ministry off the ground, I had made contact through the Internet with a girl in the Philippines.

Oddly enough, I hadn't even been thinking about preaching overseas at the time. Single guy that I was, I was hoping to meet someone nice over the worldwide web. God can use anything in your life to lead you.

I had placed my name on a Christian dating website and received a response a week later from a young lady in the Philippines named Grace. Her message was not in response to my need for companionship—she was replying in obedience to the Holy Spirit. She told me that she had come across my name and God had told her that I would be coming to her country. The Philippines was 12,500 miles away. That seemed impossible to me at the time because I was still on probation. I couldn't leave the country without special permission from the probation office, and it wasn't likely they would give permission to someone who'd been dealing drugs.

I told her it didn't seem likely that would happen, but she wasn't to be convinced otherwise. In fact, about three weeks later, I received a package from Grace containing a calendar from her church and a praise and worship tape done by her church choir. My dad was with me at the time. On the calendar was a picture of the pulpit.

When I picked up the praise and worship tape, the Lord immediately told me that He was sending me to that church. I heard Him so clearly. I was so excited that I told my dad. He laughed in disbelief and walked away. That didn't prevent me from believing. I hung the calendar on my bedroom wall and started using it.

Later, in March 1999, while at a Benny Hinn crusade in Memphis, Tennessee, I met an evangelist named Glenn Poplawski, who told me he was planning a trip to the Philippines and was looking for people to go with him. The trip would take place in September or October. I told him I knew someone in the Philippines, thinking of Grace at the time. He invited me to go on the trip with him. He wrote down my name and phone number to contact me later once he had more details about it.

After that, God took me through the transformation that led me to the Bob Shattles meetings and the meetings at Ruth Heflin's camp, which ultimately led me into full-time ministry with official credentials from Ruth Heflin's ministry.

After the time at camp, I received a phone call from Glenn Poplawski, and he confirmed that the invitation to go along on the trip was still open. I replied that I definitely wanted to go as long as God would supply the passport and the money. So, I applied for a passport, fully believing that if God had really told me I was going overseas then He would open the doors to make it possible. The judge overseeing my case responded favorably; however, my probation officer hadn't seemed to be in favor of it, so I was pleasantly surprised when the approval for the passport came through. What had seemed impossible became possible once again.

One night I was speaking with a pastor friend on the phone. As I was telling him how God was really beginning to move in my life, the power of God came over him and spoke to him. He told me the Lord had told him to pay for my plane ticket to the Philippines. Others later gave me money and everything else I needed. It was all supplied to the very penny and just in time. God had cleared away all of the obstacles.

In October, we flew to Manila in the Philippines. I had a dream that I was at a leper colony and knew right away that the dream was of God. Someone even prophesied to me that I would go to a leper colony and pray for the lepers, but it wasn't my intention to preach on this trip at all. I determined in my heart to be a servant for Glenn, who had invited me on this trip. Willingly, I took care of whatever he needed done.

Only one time did I preach and that was in a prison. But the dream and the prophecy about the leper colony wouldn't rest in my mind. By now, we were two hours north of Manila. I told Glenn that I really wanted to find a way to minister to lepers, like God had shown me in my dream. He started trying to make it happen. He tried to arrange for an airplane to one of the islands known for its leper colonies, but that fell through. The harder he tried to arrange my request, the more it seemed to fly apart. Then I told Glenn about the young lady, Grace, who lived in Manila and whom I knew through e-mail correspondence, so he thought it would be best if we headed back to Manila where I could contact her by phone.

On the airplane, Glenn mentioned that he would like to go to David Sumrall's church while we were there because he was hoping to meet him. David Sumrall was the nephew of Les Sumrall, who had helped usher in the early revivals in the Philippines some thirty-five to forty years ago. Les had established a church in Manila that was now a huge congregation, and his nephew, David, was now pastoring there.

I said, "Let's pray that it happens." We joined hands and prayed in Jesus' name that we would be able to meet David Sumrall.

Once back in Manila, I called Grace to tell her I was in the Philippines, traveling with an evangelist friend. She asked where I was. I told her we were preaching in San Fernando, Angeles City. She asked me what we planned to do while we were in Manila, because if we had the time, she was sure her pastor would like to meet us. I asked who her pastor was and she said, "David Sumrall." I hadn't known that before I called her. I contained my excitement while on the phone but as soon as I had hung up, I ran back to our room. A huge smile spread over Glenn's face as I told him the news. He was amazed, as was I, that God had begun to work out this meeting with David Sumrall ten months prior to our prayer.

To make a long story short, we met David Sumrall. I had my picture taken with him standing in the very same pulpit that was on the calendar in my bedroom back home. Then Grace helped us make the arrangements to go to a leper colony, which was really a hospital, to pray for the lepers.

The hospital was unguarded. People who saw us going in thought we were nuts. Grace had volunteered to go with us to do any interpreting that might be necessary.

There is a serious social stigma in having leprosy. Most people avoid being anywhere near someone with this disease because of the misinformation about it. Contrary to what people believe, you cannot catch leprosy from touching a leper. Jesus knew this.

We went in and had a two-hour interview with the doctor there. She couldn't believe we were there either, but she knew we were certainly not going to catch leprosy by praying for the patients.

So, we preached inside the leper colony, with interpretation by Grace, who had been the one to first tell me that God was going to bring me to the Philippines, and we prayed for the patients. Each one of the lepers who heard the Gospel that day accepted Jesus as his or her Savior.

On the plane ride home from the Philippines, as I thought about the events of the trip, I could only marvel and reflect back on my life. I had started out with the promise of the Father for great things in my life, but I had preferred to do things my own way and in the process had messed up my life. God had to break me to get my attention and to soften my heart enough to turn me around. Learning to walk with Him in trust and love had led me down the path of obedience and ultimately to fulfilling my destiny. The road had been long and hard, but now I was a full-time minister of the Gospel of Jesus Christ and I was taking that message to the nations.

CHAPTER FIFTEEN

THE BLESSINGS OF OBEDIENCE

*I do all this for the sake of the gospel, that I may share
in its blessings.*   1 Corinthians 9:23

Now that I have tasted God's goodness, given to me because of my willingness to obey Him, I have no desire for any other life. The Lord has blessed me beyond anything I ever could have imagined. I'm certainly not rich in the worldly sense, but the Lord continues to bless me in miraculous ways, such as providing the beautiful hotel room I described in the introduction of this book. That hotel room upgrade has happened to me more than once. The Lord has also blessed me with free limousine service anytime I visit New York City. A wonderful man named Tab comes to pick me up and take me anywhere I want to go. But these are just minor blessings.

The greatest blessing is that God has restored to me everything I lost through my disobedience and has given me even more. The Lord brought to me a beautiful, loving Christian wife, and we have two fabulous kids. My own daughter, Megan, now has a good relationship with her good old dad and my wife, Kecia, has a little girl, a sweetheart named Savannah. They are my greatest blessings. My prayer is that God will mold me into the world's best husband and father to my new family.

Today, I travel all over the United States as well as to other countries to share my story and the Good News about Jesus Christ, who died for us so that *we could all be blessed by God.* The Philippines and Nigeria, I mentioned in other places in this book, were just two nations that God has sent me to. I have also traveled to minister in the Ukraine, Israel, Indonesia, Japan, Malaysia, Mexico, Canada, Holland, France and Liberia. Also, Ghana has just opened up to me as I write this book.

The Lord has blessed my obedience to go anywhere He calls with an opportunity to take part in the revival that is happening in Hurley, Mississippi. I feel so blessed to be His servant there as people come to Hurley from all over the country to soak in God's presence and to receive His anointing. Pastors William and Lisa Hancock serve there as anointed vessels of God for such a time as this, and they have graciously welcomed me with open arms.

Christian television is also opening to me now as I write this book. I have been on several television stations ,and even more are opening up through worldwide satellite. God brought about this miracle through a divine appointment with two of His humble servants, Russell and Dorothy Spalding, in Augusta, Georgia. This was the couple who made the news when they walked all over America carrying the cross. The Lord blessed the Spaldings for their faithfulness by giving them a television station.

And the miracles God does through me are still happening. Just recently I was a guest on the Augusta couple's weekly television program, and as I prayed for the viewers with my hand outstretched toward the camera, God's power began to flow out into people's homes. A few of them got dressed and drove down to the station to testify. One lady told us she had been in her living room watching when the power of God literally knocked her backward off her feet and she was instantly healed of her physical problems.

Miracles continue in my meetings as well. In one service that I preached near Atlanta, there was a couple, the Argoses, who had come to visit because they had heard that God was using me to heal. The husband, Stan, was suffering from type one diabetes and had to take four insulin shots a day. When I prayed for Stan, he was miraculously healed. This would be confirmed later by his physician.

I know that greater doors than these are yet to open. This was confirmed to me in November 2002 by Pastor Benny Hinn. Kecia and I and some friends had gone to one of his miracle crusades in Charlotte, North Carolina. One of our companions was struggling with a form of cancer and was seeking healing. As God began to powerfully touch her body that night, our group was asked to come up on the platform to testify about what was happening to her. When we walked up in front of Pastor Benny, I felt as though I had walked into a pool of water and my hands instantly began to vibrate. This sensation began to spread up through my chest and all over.

Pastor Benny prayed for each of us, and when he got to me I was knocked backward through the air. I don't remember it, but others told me later that my feet flew up so high that I nearly kicked Pastor Benny. After he prayed for me a second time, he moved on to pray for some others, and as I got up and started to go back to my seat, I heard Pastor Benny calling in a loud voice, "Man of God, man of God, come back here!"

At first I thought he was calling to someone else, but when I turned to look at him he was pointing his finger right at me. I went back to the front, although not up on the platform. He began to talk to me one-on-one, and he asked me where I preached. I told him that I traveled all over America and around the world to preach. Pastor Benny told me that the Spirit of God had revealed to him that God was about to take of the Spirit that was on his life and ministry and place it on me. This was just like the Lord had instructed Moses to do when the nation of Israel was in the desert (see Numbers 11:16-17). I was excited, because I had just read that scripture passage to my brother, Scott, that same morning over the phone.

Pastor Benny then began to prophesy that God was about to double the anointing on my life and that one year from that day my ministry would be twice as big as it was then. This was confirmation of what the Lord had been telling me, that a greater anointing was about to explode our ministry. Pastor Benny then had Kecia come up to stand beside me while he prayed so he could pray for both of us. The old prophecy over my life had been fulfilled, and so the Lord gave us a new promise, a new vision and a new challenge in obedience to Him.

I would like to challenge those of you who are reading this book who have accepted Christ as your Savior but aren't experiencing God's blessings in your life. To you I would say: Examine the level of obedience you are walking out in your Christian life. What things has God called you to do that you have failed to be obedient in? Is your "engine" still stuck at the "station," going nowhere because you are still living in reluctant obedience? Are you following God's commandments and teachings only when it's comfortable and convenient? When you feel the prompting of the Holy Spirit, do you ignore Him or do you plead with Him about why you can't do what He asks? If this is the case, then God is calling you today to make a greater commitment to obey Him. Jesus, the Savior you called on for salvation, is waiting to be Lord of your life as well as your Savior. When you accept Him as Lord, you are giving up all of your rights in order to do whatever He asks of you. It's time to give up control and trust Him. He has a wonderful destiny He has designed just for you. You may not be destined to travel the world preaching the Gospel, but your personal destiny *will fulfill the desires of your heart.*

God Himself has a challenge for those of us who have surrendered to Jesus as Lord and are learning to live a life of simple obedience. We are living in unique and exciting days! Time is short and His return is close! God is calling His faithful ones to an even greater level of obedience in these last days. We need to begin to step forth into joyful obedience because this is the level of obedience we will need in order to bring in the last great move of God. Not only do we need to obey the commands of the Lord, but we need to do it out of a joyful spirit, because this is the spirit that recognizes the cost that Jesus paid. Jesus willingly laid aside His rights and His life *"for the joy set before Him,"* which was to restore all of us to a right relationship with God the Father.

Let us fix our eyes on Jesus, the author and perfecter of our faith, who for the joy set before him endured

> *the cross, scorning its shame, and sat down at the right*
> *hand of the throne of God.*   Hebrews 12:2

So you might ask, "If God tells me to go preach to lepers in Asia, I should do that joyfully?" The answer is a resounding YES! Do it for the joy of seeing those lepers receive eternal life. "If God should tell me to show love to my alcoholic father or homosexual neighbor, should I do that joyfully?" Again, the answer is YES! Do it for the joy of showing them that a life of obedience to God will benefit and bless them so much more than the lives they are living. God is calling His people to grow up and mature in their faith in these last hours of time, and joyful obedience is a hallmark of spiritual maturity.

If you have never received Jesus as your Savior, then let me assure you that reading this book is no coincidence. If you picked up this book, it's most likely because you're experiencing a broken life and you're at your point of desperation. You may have tried drugs, you may have tried alcohol, you may have tried sex, but nothing seems to fill the emptiness inside of you, and now you're desperate to find something more than the life you're living right now. The world will tell you that religion isn't the answer and so will I, because I'm not talking to you about religion. I'm talking to you about letting a living God touch your life in order to set you free from all those things that have broken you. Let Him put your feet back on the path of obedience so you can experience a life of blessing. No mistake you have made in your life is bad enough that God won't forgive it and begin using you right now.

Remember all that you have just read about my life. I was addicted to alcohol, tobacco and drugs for many years. Today, because of my surrender to Jesus as Savior and Lord and because of my willingness to live a life of obedience, I am a full-time minister of the Gospel who travels the world preaching with signs, wonders and miracles following.

The possibilities for *your* life are endless if you will simply obey Him. If you long for a better life, take that first step today, right now, and pray this prayer:

> *Lord Jesus, I need You to come into my heart and forgive all my sins. Please take out my old heart and give me a new one, one that is willing to obey You, one that thinks like You and acts like You. I surrender all of my rights to You and ask You to take over my life.*
>
> *Amen.*

David Piper Ministries
P.O. Box 174
Tifton, Georgia 31793

www.davidpiperministries.org